"A fine book . . . Phillips is a wise condenser and a good guide through the mass of relevant information and ideas—which amounts to a substantial portion of Western culture. He is able to sift from it a concise, painfully thought-provoking account of the treatment of Eve and her daughters at the hands of the sons of Adam. . . . Dazzling analytical virtuosity. . . . *Eve* is searing, admirably lucid, and deserving of a wide audience." —John Boswell, *The New York Times Book Review*

"A fascinating and devastating tale! *Eve* should be read by all concerned with equality." —Carol P. Christ, author of *Diving Deep and Surfacing* and co-editor of *Womanspirit Rising*

"Scholarly, provocative, and readable." —*Library Journal*

"Phillips discusses key themes associated with the Eve myth, including creation, fall, expiation, and redemption. The focus is on how the myth has been interpreted through the ages, and especially on how various interpretations have reflected and reinforced the culture's misogyny. . . . Highly recommended." —*Choice*.

"*Eve* is a remarkably smooth and readable study of a complex tradition." —*The Christian Century*

"Vividly explores Eve's saga." —*Philadelphia Inquirer*

"A brilliant study." —*Publishers Weekly*

"A richly documented, fast-moving feminist survey. . . stimulating and persuasive." —*Kirkus Reviews*

EVE

EVE

The History of an Idea

✝

JOHN A. PHILLIPS

1817

Harper & Row, Publishers, San Francisco
Cambridge, Hagerstown, New York, Philadelphia
London, Mexico City, São Paulo, Singapore, Sydney

FIRST HARPER & ROW PAPERBACK EDITION PUBLISHED IN 1985.

Designer: Jim Mennick

Library of Congress Cataloging in Publication Data

Phillips, John A.
    EVE, THE HISTORY OF AN IDEA.

    Bibliography: p.
    Includes index.
    I. Eve (Biblical figure)   2. Woman (Theology)
I. Title
BS580.E85P48   1984   291.2'13   83-48424
ISBN 0-06-066552-1
ISBN 0-06-250670-6 (pbk)

        86   87   88   10   9   8   7   6   5   4   3   2

for my mother
for my sister, Ann
for Jennifer and Mara, my daughters
for Deborah and Rebekah
and especially for Leona

*God made the man and the woman, and put them together.
When they saw each other, they began to laugh. Then God sent
them into the world.*

African legend

Contents

List of Illustrations ix
Preface xiii
Acknowledgments xv

I. CREATION
1. The Mother of All the Living 3
2. Pandora: The Sorrow to Men Who Eat Bread 16
3. The Lady of the Rib 25
4. The Serpent-Mother 38

II. FALL
5. The Devil's Gateway 55
6. "Mother Incest So Familiar to Us" 78

III. EXPIATION
7. "A Nail Driven into the Wall" 99
8. The "Eschatological Woman" 120

IV. REDEMPTION
9. The Second Eve 131
10. The Countertradition: Heretical Eves 148
11. Retrospect and Prospect: Eve and the Death of God 170

Notes 177
Selected Bibliography 191
Index of Authors 195
Index of Subjects 197
Index of Literature Cited in Text 201

Illustrations

Goddess, probably Aphrodite, rising from the sea; about 470 B.C. From the marble back of the *Ludovici Throne.* Sicilian or south Italian. By permission of the Museo Nazionale Romano; photograph by the Soprintendenza Archeologia di Roma. *4*

Marduk battling Tiamat. After a drawing by Lagarde of an Assyrian cylinder seal, date and provenance unknown, in Alfred Jeremias, *Das Alte Testament im Lichte des Alten Orients* (Leipzig, East Germany: 1916), p. 36. *6*

Satan, Sin and Death, by William Blake; 1808. An illustration for Milton's *Paradise Lost.* By permission of the Huntington Art Gallery, San Marino, California. *9*

Creation of Pandora, by Abraham Diepenbeeck; 1638. By permission of the Städeschen Kunstinstitut, Frankfurt am Main, West Germany. *18*

Eva Prima Pandora, by Jean Cousin; 1550. By permission of the Louvre, Paris; France photograph by Musées Nationaux. *22*

Pandora's Box as Still Life, by Paul Klee; 1920. Whereabouts unknown. Photograph by the Museum of Modern Art, New York. *24*

Creation of Eve, by Wiligelmo; 1100–1106. Duomo, Modena. Photograph by Alinari. *26*

Creation of Eve, by Jacopo della Quercia; 1425–1438. San Petronia, Bologna. Photograph by Alinari. *26*

Creation of Eve, by Michelangelo; 1511. Sistine Chapel ceiling, Vatican. Photograph by Alinari. *31*

Creation of Eve, by Lorenzo Maitani; 1310–1330. Duomo, Orvieto. Photograph by Alinari. *31*

Eve, by Albrecht Dürer; 1507. Pitti Gallery, Florence. Photograph by Alinari. *34*

Cylindrical vase with female deity; middle of the third century B.C.

By permission of the British Museum, London.   *40*

Eve, by Henri Rousseau; after 1904. By permission of the Hamburger Kunsthalle, West Germany.   *43*

Two Watchers Descending to a Daughter of Man, by William Blake; 1796. Rosenwald Collection, by permission of the National Gallery, Washington, D.C.   *48*

Angels Descending to the Daughters of Men, by John Flaxman; ca. 1821. By permission of the Fitzwilliam Museum, Cambridge, England. *48*

The bronze *Bernward Door;* ca. 1100. Hildesheim Cathedral, West Germany. Permission and photograph by J. Brüdern, Braunschweig, West Germany.   *56*

Eve and the Future: The Serpent, by Max Klinger; 1880. By permission of the Carus Gallery, New York.   *60*

Detail from *The Terrestrial Paradise,* by the Limbourg Brothers; early fifteenth century. Illustration for *Très Riches Heures du Duc de Berry.* By permission of the Musée Condé, Chantilly; photograph by Giraudon, Paris.*   *63*

Detail from *The Haywain,* triptych by Hieronymous Bosch; 1485–1490. By permission of the Prado, Madrid.   *63*

Detail from *Adam and Eve,* detail by Pseudo Met de Bles; first half of the sixteenth century. Pinacoteca, Bologna. Photograph by Alinari.   *63*

The Temptation, by Jacopo della Quercia; 1425–1438. S. Petronio, Bologna. Photograph by Alinari.   *65*

Temptation of Eve, by William Blake; 1808. Illustration for Milton's *Paradise Lost.* By permission of the Boston Museum of Fine Arts. *66*

Adam, by Filippino Lippi; 1502. Santa Maria Novella, Florence. Photograph by Alinari.   *68*

Detail from *Temptation and Expulsion,* by Michelangelo; 1511. Sistine Chapel ceiling, Vatican. Photograph by Alinari.   *69*

Detail from *Temptation and Expulsion,* by Michelangelo; 1511. Sistine Chapel ceiling, Vatican. Photograph by Alinari.   *71*

Expulsion from Paradise, by Masaccio; ca. 1425. Santa Maria Novella, Florence. Photograph by Alinari.   *71*

---

*This and the two paintings that follow show the serpent as Eve's double.

Cupid Complaining to Venus, by Lucas Cranach, 1529. By permission of the National Gallery, London. *73*

Adam, Eve and Satan, by Michelangelo Naccherino; 1550–1622. Boboli Gardens, Florence. Photograph by Alinari. *75*

Adam and Eve, by Max Beckmann; 1932. By permission, private collection.* *82*

Adam and Eve, by Hans Baldung Grien; 1511. Rosenwald Collection; by permission of the National Gallery of Art, Washington, D.C. *86*

Adam and Eve, by Max Beckmann, 1917. By permission, private collection. *86*

Parua na te Varua Ino ("Words of the Evil Spirit"), by Paul Gauguin; 1892. By permission of the National Gallery of Art, Washington, D.C. *88*

Adam and Eve, by Hans Baldung Grien; 1519. Rosenwald Collection; by permission of the National Gallery of Art, Washington, D.C. *92*

Breton Eve, by Paul Gauguin; 1889. Bequest of Marion Koogler McNay; by permission of the Marion Koogler McNay Art Institute, San Antonio, Texas. *94*

Detail from the *Sarcophagus of Junius Bassus;* fourth century. Vatican Museum. Photograph by Alinari. *100*

Adam and Eve, by Lucas Cranach; 1526. Lee Collection; by permission of the Courtauld Institute, London. *103*

Adam and Eve, by Rembrandt; 1638. Rosenwald Collection; by permission of the National Gallery of Art, Washington, D.C. *107*

The Fall, by Mabuse (Jan Gossaert); after 1510. Detail from the Malvagna Triptych, Museo, Palermo, Sicily. Photograph by Alinari. *111*

Eve, by Antonio Rizzo; 1465–1485. Doge's Palace, Venice. Photograph by Alinari. *116*

Adam and Eve, detail from *The Ghent Altarpiece*, by Hubert and Jan van Eyck; completed 1432. St. Bavo, Ghent, Belgium. Photo-

---

*This and the following painting illustrate confusion of the forbidden fruit with Eve's breast.

graph and permission by the Institut Royal du Patrimonie Artistique, Brussels, Belgium.   *119*

Temptation of Eve, by Gislebertus; ca. 1130. By permission of the
Musée Rolin, Ste. Lazare, Autun, France. Photograph by G.
Varlez.   *122*

Eve, detail from *Christ in Limbo*, by Sodoma; 1517. Pinacoteca,
Siena. Photograph by Alinari.   *125*

Detail from *The Creation of Adam*, by Michelangelo; 1511. Sistine
Chapel ceiling, Vatican. Photograph by Alinari.   *134*

Schuetzmantel-Maria aus Ravensburg, by Michael Erhart; ca. 1480. By
permission of the Staatliche Museen Preussicher Kultur Besitz, W.
Berlin. Photograph by J. P. Anders.   *137*

The Great Red Dragon and the Woman Clothed with the Sun, by William
Blake; ca. 1805. From the Rosenwald Collection; by permission
of the National Gallery of Art, Washington, D.C.   *141*

An Islamic Adam and Eve, by Manafi al-Hayawan; 1294–1299. Maragha, Iran. By permission of the Pierpont Morgan Library, New
York.   *151*

Illustration from *Chronology of Ancient Peoples*, by al-Biruni; 1307–
1308, Iran. By permission of the University of Edinburgh Library.
155

Eve and the Serpent, by William Blake; undated. By permission of the
Victoria and Albert Gallery, London.   *156*

Where Do We Come From? Who Are We! Where Are We Going? by Paul
Gauguin; 1897. By permission of the Boston Museum of Fine
Arts.   *163*

Eve, by Emil Nolde; 1910. Hagemann Collection, by permission of
the Städelsches Museum, Frankfurt am Main, West Germany.
173

Preface

The story of Eve is, in a sense, at the heart of the concept of Woman in Western civilization. In the Genesis story, she is the most important character in the drama enacted in the Garden of Eden. Her actions precipitate the fall from unity and harmony with God into estrangement and sin; into the human condition of sexual consciousness and conscience, as well as the hard realities of birth, work, and death. But her story does not end there. She is also Everywoman, the prototypical woman, all of her sex who are yet to come. And, as Everywoman, her actions in Genesis cause her to be regarded in Western religions as a special problem, requiring special measures for the working out of her salvation.

Eve is thus a living part of the cultural and social histories of the people touched by her characterization in Genesis. Her story, along with other stories, other images, other ideas, shapes a Western ideology of women. Through the developing history of this theme, continually reworked and retold not only in theology but also in art, music, literature, law, and social custom, the nature and destiny of Woman in the Western world is disclosed. To follow the path of Eve is to discover much about the identity that has been imposed upon women in Western civilization. If one would understand Woman, one must come to terms with Eve.

But which Eve? Modern biblical scholarship regards most earlier interpretations of Eve as prime examples of *eisegesis*—that is, the reading into the text of the interpreter's own ideas and prejudices. The real Eve is the Eve of Genesis, and a faithful exegesis of the scriptural story, one that concentrates on the historical, literary, and theological meaning of the verses themselves and refuses to impose a particular view of the nature and destiny of Woman upon them, will disclose her. The history of the interpretation of Eve, modern scholars hold, is largely a history of misunderstanding and malice and has little to offer in understanding the Eve of Genesis.

Assuming that the true Eve, were she to be found, would really be so different from the others, the contemporary scholars' claim to objectivity must raise a particular problem for the faithful. The Talmud, Qur'an, *hadith,* and the New Testament and Christian dogma have intervened between interpreter and text to impress particular religious interpretations on the verses of Genesis. If readers are Christians, Jews, or Muslims, they have already had the story of Eve read for them. These readings, when set alongside any objective reading of the Genesis text, prove to be a part of the history of the misinterpretation of Eve. To insist that we simply discover and then restrict ourselves to the original intent of the Genesis writer is to challenge the integrity of religious tradition and the unity and authority of the Word.

One can argue that just such a challenge is necessary for church, mosque, and synagogue; and attempting to disclose the sense of the author freed from tendentious interpretation is one aim of this study. But for an understanding of Western culture, examining the history of the misinterpretation of Eve is more important. It is the misinterpreted Eve, and not the Eve of modern scholarship, who has played the significant role in the drama of history. In our exegesis of the prototypical woman of Western civilization, it is more important to set the Eve of Western religion in her place as a part of the history of an idea than to rescue the real Eve from the misreading of her story.

Our prospect, then, is to interpret the interpretations and to exegete the exegeses. This study must analyze motifs and—because this is necessarily a moral history—motivations. We will pay close attention to the heretical, the heterodox, when it reveals the true face of the orthodox itself or suggests a way out of a dilemma. We will also turn methodologies back upon their practitioners and ask at each turn: Why is it so important for this theologian or that poet, this artist or that psychoanalyst, to retell the story in just this way? And when we come to the end of this story of Eve in the Western tradition, we must ask whether there is any way out for her.

Acknowledgments

As I have collected the material for this book over the years, I have accumulated many debts—some to people who have no doubt since forgotten exactly what it was they said or did. From some I received scholarly or editorial assistance, from others much-needed encouragement, and from still others a friendship that taught me about the nature of men and women. I wish to thank the following people for their particular contributions:

Nor Hall, Lowell Christy, Albert Hofstader, Maria Pinedo, Bert Kaplan, Charolette London, Jean Wharton, Joe Allen, Hal Hargreaves, Ruth Mercer, Stephan Lachmann, Lydia McCoy, Noel King, Marlene Bunch, William Hamilton, Louise Preble, Ron Marshall, Cheryl Doering, Tom Idinopulos, Leo Steinberg, Babette Bohn, Carol Christ, and Murray Baumgarten.

Whether to support some contention of my own or to disagree with them, I have at times leaned more heavily than is customary on the work of Paul Schwarz, J. M. Evans, Marina Warner, Leo Steinberg, John Bugge, and Robin Scroggs. I wish to express my thanks.

I. CREATION

When God began to create the heaven and the earth—the earth being unformed and void, with darkness over the surface of the deep and a wind from God sweeping over the water—God said, "Let there be light"; and there was light. God saw that the light was good, and God separated the light from the darkness. God called the light Day, and the darkness he called Night. And there was evening and there was morning, a first day. God said, "Let there be an expanse in the midst of the water, that it may separate water from water." God made the expanse, and it separated the water which was below the expanse from the water which was above the expanse. And it was so.

GEN. 1:1-7

And God said, "Let us make man in our image, after our likeness. They shall rule the fish of the sea, the birds of the sky, the cattle, the whole earth, and all the creeping things that creep on earth." And God created man in his image, in the image of God he created him; male and female he created them. God blessed them and God said to them, "Be fertile and increase, fill the earth and master it; and rule the fish of the sea, the birds of the sky, and all the living things that creep on earth."

GEN. 1:26-28

The LORD God said, "It is not good for man to be alone; I will make a fitting helper for him." And the LORD God formed out of the earth all the wild beasts and all the birds of the sky, and brought them to the man to see what he would call them; and whatever the man called each living creature, that would be its name. And the man gave names to all the cattle and to the birds of the sky and to all the wild beasts; but for Adam no fitting helper was found. So the LORD God cast a deep sleep upon the man; and while he slept, he took

one of his ribs and closed up the flesh at that spot. And the
LORD God fashioned the rib that he had taken from the man
into a woman; and he brought her to the man.

Then the man said,

> "This one at last
> Is bone of my bones
> And flesh of my flesh.
> This one shall be called Woman,
> For from man was she taken."

GEN. 2:18-23

The man named his wife Eve, because she was the mother of
all the living.

GEN. 3:20

1. The Mother of All the Living

The earliest answers to the great question of "Whence?" all reiterate, in various forms, the same idea: it was out of the body of the primordial goddess that the world-egg emerged or that the earth was born; or alternately, it was the goddess' body itself that provided the material from which the earth was made. Thus the oldest cosmogonies, like the oldest worship of concretely represented deities, typically start with a primal goddess.[1]*

The Mother Goddess of ancient Near Eastern religions, by whatever name she was called, was honored and worshiped with the title "the Mother of All the Living." According to Genesis, this is the meaning of *Ḥawwāh*, or Eve, the name given by Adam to the first woman. Although the writers of Genesis "completely demythologize the function of the goddess"[2] so that she appears simply as a woman, Eve is related by her name to humanity's earliest attempts to articulate the nature of Woman, the Feminine as a religious concept, and the very origins of human consciousness of the sacred. "Behind the character of Eve," says Isaac Kikawada, "was probably hidden the figure of the creatress or Mother Goddess."[3] Eve's history, Scripture insists, is the story of a mere woman, albeit the first woman. But the story of Eve is also the story of the displacing of the Goddess whose name is taken from a form of the Hebrew verb "to be" by the masculine God, Yahweh, whose name has the same derivation.[4] We cannot understand the history of Eve without seeing her as a deposed Creator-Goddess, and indeed, in some sense as creation itself. The first woman "receives some of the attributes of the creatress in addition to the character of the created, and thereby a transparent image is superimposed upon her."[5] In Genesis, it is the

---

* Reference notes begin on page 177.

Goddess, probably Aphrodite, rising from the sea; about 470 B.C. From the marble back of the *Ludovici Throne*, Sicilian or south Italian. By permission of the Museo Nazionale Romano; photograph by the Soprintendenza Archeologia di Roma.

masculine Yahweh who creates the world, and not the Mother of All the Living. What does this mean about Eve's transparent image and her history?

※

The great creation stories of ancient Near Eastern cultures have at least two important things in common: All deal with the initiation and sustenance of human civilization, the securing of religious and cosmological foundations for the *polis;* and all presuppose or describe power struggles between masculine and feminine deities, usually with the masculine deities eventually gaining the upper hand. It is as though the writers believed that civilization could not begin or be sustained until the Feminine, as a dominant religious power, had been mastered and domesticated. We know that this is what happened at the dawn of Greek civilization, as the powerful female and benign male consort deities were supplanted by the successively more masculine regimes of the Uranians and Olympians. Gods who created replaced goddesses who procreated and controlled the cycles of birth and death and the seasons.

Similarly, the Mesopotamian saga of creation, the *Enûma elish,* narrates the destruction of the terrible Tiamat, the dragon-mother of all creation, in the cataclysmic struggle with Marduk, the young warrior-god who has taken for himself the potency and fealty of the other deities. When at last he has defeated the treacherous Tiamat, he creates the world by splitting her carcass into earth and sky; she herself becomes the primordial matter of the universe.[6] Creation stories from the Near East

begin, as a rule, with a theogony, that is, with the origin of the gods, the genealogy of the deities who preceded the birth of the world and mankind; and they tell of the antagonism between this god and that god, of friction that arose from these clashes of will, and of mighty wars that were waged by the gods. They connected the genesis of the world with the genesis of the gods and with the hostilities and wars between them; and they identified the different parts of the universe with given deities or with certain parts of their bodies.[7]

Most Old Testament scholars, however, say that this is not the case with the creation story in Genesis. In the opening verses, however, we find the statement that the world was *tohu-wa-bohu,* "unformed and void." *Tohu* is related to the Hebrew loan word *tehom,* the "deeps" or heavenly ocean-chaos that is held back by the "expanse" (what the King James Version calls the "firmament") so that it might not destroy all creation; *Tehom* in turn is related to *Tiamat,* the formless, dark, menacing female of *Enûma elish.*[8] Somewhere in the back of the minds of the writers of Genesis is the Tiamat world of dark and storm, and the story of the masculine warrior-god who creates the cosmos from out of chaos, splitting the dragon-mother's corpse as the initial act of creation. The transparent image of Marduk is thus superimposed upon Yahweh.

The theology of Genesis, however, cannot admit primordial struggles between deities because there are no deities to struggle; God is one and he alone is divine. Moreover, the material out of which he creates the universe is not himself, or any other divine material. He creates out of "nothing"—neutral stuff that has no religious

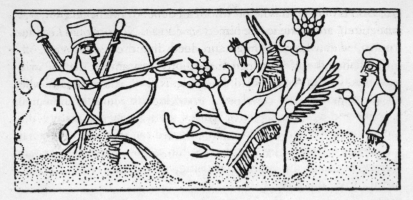

Marduk battling Tiamat. In one of her appendages she holds a crescent moon, an ancient symbol for the Goddess. After a drawing by Lagarde of an Assyrian cylinder seal, date and provenance unknown, in Alfred Jeremias, *Das Alte Testament im Lichte des Alten Orients* (Leipzig, East Germany: 1916), p. 36.

identity. Jewish and Christian theologies both insist upon *creatio ex nihilo,* maintaining that contrary to the teaching of the *Enûma elish,* God cannot be confused with his world; he is substantially distinct from it. The mythology of the Bible thus undercuts the presupposition of earlier myths of the interpenetration of human and divine. God and humanity do not merge in the Bible; they stand independently and make covenants with each other.

✳

Unlike many deities of the ancient Near East, the God of Israel shared his power with no female divinity, nor was he the divine husband or lover of any. He can scarcely be characterized in any but masculine epithets: king, lord, master, judge and father. Indeed, the absence of feminine symbolism for God marks Judaism, Christianity and Islam in striking contrast to the world's other religious traditions.[9]

Genesis holds as incontrovertible and irreducible the dictum of Hebraic religion that God is one: "Hear, O Israel, Yahweh our God, Yahweh is One" (Deut. 6:4); "I am God, and beside me there is no other" (Isa. 45:5). The Qur'an is equally unequivocal: "Say:

He, God is one. God is he on whom all depend. He begets not, nor is begotten, and none is like him" (*Sūra* 112). Not only has God no consort, with whom he might produce divine or semidivine offspring, but his self-contained masculinity guarantees that he will have no sexual life of any kind. He "begets not"; it is goddesses who beget. Built into the concept of goddesses is actual or potential plurality. Genesis does not even preface its story of creation with the refutation of the notion of plural deities; its writers assume that God is one and therefore male, male and therefore one. Its writers may be said to be a step beyond the *Enûma elish* in the religious revolution; here it is taken for granted that the Goddess is dead, and there is no sanguine precreation story to even tell of her demise. Nor does she live on in some other form, as a vitiated universe or demigoddess, for example. For accounts of divine struggles among the dieties, the writers of Genesis substitute the story of the creation itself. What other religions regarded as deities are dethroned and presented as mere creatures—sun, moon, stars, plants, animals, and people. Even in male-dominated religious systems, female deities were often retained and their worship sanctioned, but not in this case. Eruptions of Goddess worship (and its attendant temple prostitution) are proscribed as idolatry. God is one, and to secure his oneness, God is male.

Thus the Old Testament cannot suggest that there are other divinities with whom humanity might have to deal; there is only God. Nevertheless, what is not permissible as doctrine is allowed to be expressed in the poetry of ancient liturgy, where it serves to remind us of Yahweh's power. Yahweh continually struggles against evil personified as female forces and powers: Tehom (Tiamat), Rahab, and Leviathan (Lothan), all names for the chaotic dragon in Mesapotamian and Canaanite tradition.

> Was it not thou that didst cut Rahab in pieces,
>   Thou that didst pierce the dragon?
> Was it not thou that didst dry up the sea,
>   The waters of the great Tehom? (ISA. 51:9-10)

> Thou didst divide the sea by thy might;
>   Thou didst break the heads of the dragons on the waters;

Thou didst crush the heads of Leviathan,
　Thou didst give him as food for the creatures. (PS. 74:15-17)

By his power he stilled Tehom
　By his understanding he smote Rahab,
By his wind the heavens were made fair;
　His hand pierced the fleeing serpent. (JOB 26:12-13)

Thou dost rule the raging of Tehom;
　When its waves rise, thou stillest them.
Thou didst crush Rahab like a carcass,
　Thou didst scatter thy enemies with thy mighty arm. (PS. 89:9-12)

Such passages—and there are many of them—demonstrate the indebtedness to Babylonian and Canaanite mythology that is only hinted at in the rigidly monotheistic text of Genesis.[10] More important, such imagery serves to demonstrate the seriousness with which the masculine character of God is taken. Yahweh is a warrior who must time and again do battle against the evil dragon-mother. Like Marduk, Yahweh guards his universe against eruptions of that chaotic power that constantly threatens to undo the work of creation. Because of the singleminded concentration of Hebrew theology on God's oneness, the powers that dare to stand against God can be given religious statement only in the poetry of worship. But there the old myth is allowed to reassert itself. Tiamat opens her mouth to swallow Marduk back into her body; Tehom threatens Yahweh with the undoing of creation, with destruction, with nonbeing. Thus again and again in Jewish and Christian history, God's agents, his angels or saints, must ride forth to meet the dragon of chaos, disorder, sin, or "Error":

But full of fire and greedy hardiment,
The youthful knight could not for ought be staide,
But forth into the darksome hole he went,
And looked in: his glistering armor made
A little glooming light, much like a shade,
By which he saw the ugly monster plaine,
Halfe like a serpent horribly displaide,
But th'other halfe did woman's shape retaine,
Most lothsom, filthie, foule and full of vile disdaine.

And as she lay upon the durtie ground,
Her huge long taile her den all overspred,

Satan, Sin and Death, by William Blake; 1808. An illustration for Milton's
Paradise Lost. Blake's frequent association of women with dragons or serpents, and with evil and the demonic, is in keeping with the old religious
tradition. By permission of the Huntington Art Gallery, San Marino, California.

> Yet was in knots and many boughtes upwound,
> Pointed with mortall sting. Of her there bred
> A thousand yong ones, which she dayly fed,

Sucking upon her poisnous dugs, each one
Of sundrie shapes, yet all ill favored:
Soone as that uncouth light upon them shone,
Into her mouth they crept, and suddain all were gone.[11]

"Still that ancient foe doth seek to work us woe." Here in Spenser's poetry is the transparent image of the deposed goddess, as portrayed by the victor; the ideology of women as unstable, threatening, in league with underworld powers, secretive, and sexually uncontrollable. The story and character of Tiamat casts a long shadow over the story and character of the first woman.

✳

It is by now a common complaint of feminist religious scholars that the Old Testament not only reflects the Near Eastern mythology of cosmic struggles between a male warrior-deity and a female deity, but also bears witness to the same kind of society. That is, a culture that worships a victorious male God is a patriarchal culture. The Old Testament concept of God "deifies" sexism by giving religious authenticity to a sociopolitical system.

In an attempt to rehabilitate the Old Testament God on behalf of feminism, however, Phyllis Trible argues the contrary: "The nature of the God of Israel *defies* sexism."[12] The biblical conception of God is essentially liberating and antithetical to sexism, Trible asserts, but the patriarchal society of ancient Israel conceptualized this God to reflect its own structure. Disclosing the true biblical God thus becomes a problem of interpretation that requires what Trible terms a "depatriarchalizing" exegesis.

But is such a separation of "essence" from what is nonessential, the "kernel from the husk," really possible? It should already be clear that while Yahweh, like Marduk before him and Allah after him, may assume traditionally female attributes and titles, he cannot *be* female. He liberates as a male. To conceive of him otherwise is to remove the linchpin from a fundamental assumption of biblical theology. We must therefore address ourselves to the question of the male identity of the God of the Old Testament and see what transparent image falls upon his human counterpart, Adam.

Because the Old Testament is so insistent that God is "not man," any discussion of masculine or feminine characteristics of God must begin with the proviso that strictly speaking, he has neither. "To say that God is either male or female is . . . completely impossible from the viewpoint of traditional Judaism."[13] Yet he is traditionally and almost exclusively depicted as male when it is necessary to describe him. Is this simply a convenient anthropomorphism, rendering God humanly apprehensible while recognizing that he is finally incomprehensible?

It appears to be more than this. "The biblical God-concept, intuitively grasped by the prophets and gropingly reached by the people, reflects the strictly patriarchal order of the society which produced it; this patriarchal society gave rise to a religion centered around a single, universal deity whose will was embodied in the Law, but who was abstract, devoid of all physical attributes and yet pronouncedly male, a true projection of the patriarchal family-head."[14] It seems to be essential, not accidental, that God is depicted as male. The proper names for God, Yahweh and Elohim, are masculine in form, and adjectives that describe him and verbs that indicate his activities are masculine as well. Pronouns related to him are masculine pronouns. He acts, almost always, as a man acts. He is king, husband, father, and lord of battles, and his masculinity as depicted in the Old Testament carries over to the Talmud.

It is also the case that in the minds of the writers of the Old Testament, he *must* be depicted as male if he is to have a covenant with Israel.

Yahweh's covenant with Israel is a covenant with those competent to enter into such a thing; that is to say, with the men: they represent the people. Woman has no place in this revelation, therefore she is a constant danger to the worship of Yahweh. The Decalogue addresses the man only. . . . The male is man, and the people of Israel consists of men.[15]

The reverse, of course, must also be true: Israel's covenant with Yahweh is a covenant with one competent to enter into such a thing —a male God. But the familiar argument that the maleness of God in the Bible is the reflection of a patriarchal society seeking legitimization for the subjugation of women, is not as important as a less remarked upon characteristic of a God who is both male and one:

He cannot procreate. The Old Testament wished to establish that
Yahweh is related to his world in a manner entirely different from
the way deities related to the world in the ancient theologies. It is
not incidental that the concept of nature, traditionally associated
with goddesses, is totally absent in the Old Testament.[16] Yahweh's
realm is not nature but history. The God of Judaism is a god whose
character it is to act. He is, it is true, the Creator and, as such, Lord
of nature; but he creates by acting, by speaking, by bringing into
being. He does not, cannot, function as a Creator-Goddess; nature
and procreation cannot be an extension of his divinity. Yahweh is

not a deity associated with nature and identified with it wholly or in part,
but a God who stands absolutely above nature, and outside of it, and nature
and all its constituent elements, even the sun and all the other entities, be
they ever so exalted, are only his creations, made according to his will.[17]

Time and again the people of Israel turned to the Canaanite deities
to perform the mysteries associated with agriculture because they
could not believe that these could be performed by Yahweh; time
and again Yahweh had to assert his power over this realm.

It was I who gave her the grain, the wine, and the oil, and who lavished
upon her silver and gold which they used for Ba'al (Hos. 1:8).

As H. Wheeler Robinson asserts, "The conception of the God
who works in history is inseparably linked to his manifestation in
natural phenomena. He is what Nature, as well as history, reveals
him to be, and Nature is his peculiar language."[18] But the creation
language of Genesis is not the language of nature. It is the language
of craftsmanship, or better, recognizing what craftsmanship actually
represented in the ancient world, it is the language of *technology.* [19]
God molds, shapes, and forms the world and its creatures, just as a
potter at the wheel pushes a shapeless mass into a shape in harmony
with the potter's will and imagination. God "separates" (a word
used in the craft of leather cutting) light from darkness and the
heavenly from the earthly waters. He places above the earth an
"expanse" (or "firmament"), borrowing from smithing a Hebrew
word used for a hammered strip of metal. When his creation is
complete he pronounces it "good," that is, "sound," just as a
Mesopotamian craftsman did, as required by law, before a product

left the shop. Even humanity is not of God's body, but rather is fashioned by the divine potter from a clod of earth and given the name *adamah* ("clod") as a reminder of origin. God is not "in" humanity and he is not "in" the world. The world and all that is in it is the work of his fingers, but in no sense his offspring.

The more sophisticated account of creation in Chapter 1 of Genesis—traditionally called the Priestly account—carries out its masculinizing of the relationship between God and his world on another level. God does not even handle his raw material; instead, he "speaks" his creation into being. His realm is the realm of the spoken, his Word. The Priestly writer seems to assume that if the relationship of God to the world were that of mother to child, or even divine potter to clay figure, the historical world would be without religious foundation. Creation, unlike procreation, depends on conceptualizing. There thus appears to be a more than coincidental relationship between the beginning of history—the writing of epic creation myths as the religious foundation of civilization—and the notably antifeminine plot of such myths. The beginning of civilization seems to require a seizure of religious power by male gods, in order to break the ties of humanity to blood, soil, and nature.

As craftsman-technician and wordsmith,[20] God the Father assumes the place of the Mother of All the Living. The God of Genesis thus carries forward the religious revolution begun with the *Enûma elish*. It is the Babylonian Marduk who challenges the power of the procreative parent and initiates the liberation of humanity from its bondage to blood, soil, and nature. But Marduk's world is still a religious world, a world not created by, but nonetheless created from, the body of the Goddess, over whom Marduk must still maintain close watch. Babylonian humanity is not only *in* the world, it is still part of its quasi-divine substance. According to Genesis, the world is not procreated, nor "of one substance" with the Mother Goddess, but rather "created out of nothing." Humanity thus need have no religious attitude toward the world. The biblical writers thus "de-divinize" the world in conceiving of it as "sheer world," to use two expressions of the late Ronald Gregor Smith. Yahweh does not relate to the world in a sexual, bodily, religious mode, but relates to it instead as its craftsman. He is distinct from his creation, but as his handiwork it is precious to him. As craftsman, technician, or wordsmith, God's purpose is to conceptualize a plan and carry it out. Humanity is to fill the earth and have dominion over it, yet not worship it or anything in it. Since God is not tied to nature, his special creation, humanity, is liberated from birth, procreation, and the finality of death, may itself build and do. In short, humanity can at last have a history—and the alienation that accompanies it.[21]

The Old Testament writers attempt to soften the severity of this alienation by asserting Yahweh's interest in areas associated with the Goddess's realm of procreation, and by attributing traditionally feminine characteristics to him: pity, mercy, and a motherly attitude toward his children. Even though the Holy Land and the Jews are not divine, Israel is nonetheless depicted as God's spouse (Isa. 50: 1-8, 62:1-5; Jer. 2:2-3, 20-25; 3:1-20; Hos. 1-4, 14). Yahweh is husband as well as father, capable of spousal love and demanding obedience. But there can be no sexual relationship between Yahweh and his people. Procreation and parenting have been replaced with lordship and covenant.

An early Jewish elaboration of the account of the separation of the upper from the lower waters in Genesis 1 held that God had separated lovers locked in copulative embrace, who continue to cry out to be allowed to return to their pleasure.[22] But biblical religion, and the conception of God at its center, must, as both Augustine and Freud recognized, temper human sexual expression on behalf of civilized history. To civilize is to be in need of salvation (or sublimate), and to be in need is to be religious (or neurotic). History is a nightmare, and primitive comfort, the womb, with Mother Nature at the beginning and end of history, is what humanity longs for. Civilization is a kind of *coitus interruptus* for the sake of getting the work done. As Claus Westermann points out, the sequential history of Genesis does not really concern a series of actual events leading from a state of primal bliss to a fall from grace. It is not a movement from creation to Fall, because humans never really change. It is, instead, an account of the way things are, of humanity in the world. Humans are made that way, they are created like God, and their fall makes them like God. Because of the Fall, they know what God knows, but of course they always knew what God knows. The Fall is the natural outcome of creation.[23]

The history of Eve begins with the appearance of Yahweh in the place of the Mother of All the Living. This shift of power marks a fundamental change in the relationship between humanity and God, the world and God, the world and humanity, and men and women. The continued life of Tiamat in the liturgy of the Bible attests to humanity's ambivalent feelings about the religious revolution set in motion by the writers of *Enûma elish* and carried through by the writers of Genesis. That ambivalence, the shadow of the dethroned Goddess and the rejection of the Feminine as a sacred entity, will attend us as we take up the history of the first woman.

2. *Pandora: The Sorrow to Men Who Eat Bread*

> Whatever the Life-Goddess Eve was originally like, she appears in Genesis as a Hebrew Pandora, the villainess in a story about the origin of human misfortune. . . . She has dwindled to being merely the first woman, a troublemaker, created from a rib of the senior and dominant first man.[1]

The Church Fathers drew on three sources in attempting to understand the third chapter of Genesis. They were certainly aware of the testimony of several nonscriptural Jewish writings, especially *The Secrets of Enoch, The Apocalypse of Moses,* and *The Books of Adam and Eve,* which had been translated into Greek and which present a particularly negative view of Eve's character and actions.[2] The second source was the New Testament, which in epistles attributed to Paul cites passages in Genesis in defense of the view that women should be subordinate to men.[3] The third source, oddly enough, was the pagan story of Pandora, which seems to have both repelled and fascinated the earliest Christian theologians. As apologists for the faith, they were obliged to come to terms with it; as Christians, they had to reject its claims. But as teachers and moralists, they could not seem to let the story go.

⁂

Hesiod's *Works and Days* tells us that Zeus, angry at Prometheus for the theft of fire, directs Hephaistos to fashion the first woman out of clay so that she might be sent to Prometheus as punishment:

As the price of fire I will give them an evil,
            and all men shall fondle
   this, their evil, close to their hearts,
            and take delight in it.[4]

The craftsman-god creates her in the image of the goddesses, each of whom, along with the gods, gives her a particular attribute—hence her name Pandora ("all gifts"). Along with her beauty and grace, which are to be "a snare to men,"[5] she is provided with "the mind of a hussy, and a treacherous nature,"[6] "lies, and wheedling words of falsehood,"[7] so that she will prove "a sorrow to men who eat bread."[8]

When she is completed, she is spurned by the suspicious Prometheus ("forethought"), who also warns his brother Epimetheus ("afterthought") not to accept any presents from Zeus. Nevertheless, Epimetheus marries her. After a time, she removes the lid of a mysterious jar (a *pithos* or large, stationary vessel used in ancient Greece for both storage and burial purposes) which turns out to contain "troubles by thousands" from which humanity had hitherto been free. When it is finally closed, only hope remains imprisoned under the lid of the great jar. Thus, whether through stupidity, malice, complicity with Zeus, or simple curiosity, the first woman is made responsible for the presence in the world of illness and death, miseries of all kinds, the vices, and sin.

It is quite likely, judging from the text, that Hesiod worked with fragments of traditional stories out of which he could not make complete sense, and which he put together in his own way, for his own purposes. Does Zeus intend that the woman herself should constitute the punishment, or that it should come through some action on her part? The account of her creation depicts her as an evil even before she has released any of the troubles from the jar. Zeus says that he intends to "give men . . . an evil thing in which they may all be glad of heart while they embrace their own destruction,"[9] "a beautiful evil [*kalòn kakón*] to be the price of the blessing."[10] Then what of the jar? It is introduced into the story abruptly, without adequate explanation, and one can only suppose that it has long been a fixture in the household of Epimetheus. Does he know of its origin

Creation of Pandora, by Abraham Diepenbeeck; 1638. Hermes, reaching toward Pandora with his staff, is evident among the gods. By permission of the Städeschen Kunstinstitut, Frankfurt am Main, West Germany.

and what it contains? Does Pandora? Had she been told by Zeus to open it, or by her husband not to? Is hope trapped in it so that it might remain hidden among humanity, someday to be released, or so that it will be kept from humanity forever? The story does not give us the answers.

All in all, the tale is told in such an untidy fashion and with such pointedly antifeminist asides that it is difficult not to agree with Robert Graves's charge that "Hesiod's account . . . is not genuine myth, but an antifeminist fable, probably of his own invention. . . . The pessimist Hesiod blames her for man's mortality and all the ills which beset life, as well as for the frivolous and unseemly behavior of wives."[11] But the story does reflect, however distorted, genuine myth; it parallels the story of creation and alienation in Genesis. It is Hermes, the trickster god, who gives Pandora her voice, her name, and her feminine wiles, playing a role reminiscent of the serpent in the garden of Eden. Hermes was also the deity closest to Pandora, and it is worth reminding ourselves of some of his characteristics. His function was to upset established order. He was highly erotic; his symbol was the phallus, and his son was Pan, the epitome of sexual desire who became a primary source for the Christian conception of the Devil. Both Hermes and Pan were chthonic gods, related to the underworld as the place of death and fertility.[12]

Epimetheus is said to recognize that Pandora is evil only after he has "taken possession" of her, that is, they have had intercourse; eros is thus an underlying theme of the story. The notion of eros as a theme is reinforced for those who draw a parallel between the opening of the jar and the eating of the fruit in the creation story of Genesis. In the story of Pandora and in Genesis, the result of the introduction of Woman into the world is the same: The earth is changed from a paradise into a problematic place where hard labor, birth, and death are facts of life.[13]

Additional probing into the origin of the story of Pandora further validates the idea that the story is genuine myth. Schopenhauer and modern commentators have championed alternate readings by Philodemus and Babrius which, though written much later than Hesiod's seem to preserve more ancient tradition. These renditions relate that it was Epimetheus, or simply Man, who opened the fateful vessel out of simple curiosity, releasing not evils but virtues that henceforth have eluded human grasp.[14] It is also unclear whether the name Pandora is derived from the bestowal of dubious gifts (thus "all gifts") or as "giver of all"—one of the titles by which the Greek goddess Rhea was worshiped. Hesiod himself seems to suggest this connection. With a voice suddenly grown worshipful, he tells in *Theogony* of a marvelous crown fashioned by Hephaistos for Pandora:

> On this had been done much intricate work,
>   a wonder to look at:
> Wild animals, such as the mainland
>   and the sea also produce
> In numbers, and he put many on,
>   the imitations of living
> Things, that have voices, wonderful,
>   and it flashed in its beauty.[15]

That the *pithos,* which functioned as a jar for preservation or burial, was a powerful religious symbol for the female deity at a time when feminine rather than masculine motifs may have dominated Greek culture is well documented in Neumann's study.[16] Perhaps we should see Pandora as the Mother Goddess herself, as the jar in which life is created and sustained, and which then receives the dead. There is a tantalizing hint that one version of the story that predated Hesiod's presented a man or woman with two jars, one containing *kalòn* ("good") and the other *kakón* ("evil"), and left humanity to choose. By Hesiod's time, or perhaps by his own hand, the two jars had become one and Pandora herself had become a *kalòn kakón.*[17]

In any event, and as the renowned classicist Jane Harrison always claimed, Hesiod seems to be promoting the primarily masculine interests of the Olympian gods by distorting and misrepresenting stories inherited from a more ancient worship favorable to women.[18] According to Greek mythology, the Olympians were the third generation of gods and goddesses; they came to power when Zeus emasculated and banished his father, Cronos. There is a corresponding assumption of the functions of his mother, Rhea, by his negatively characterized wife and sister, Hera. The story of Pandora, in Hesiod's rendition, reflects this trend and becomes an *apologia* for the social subordination of women. From Pandora, in Hesiod's view, "originates the breed of female women, and they live with mortal men, and are a great sorrow to them"; "therefore do not let any sweet-talking woman beguile your good sense with the fascinations of her shape. It's your barn she's after."[19]

Folklorists have been unable to agree on the correct classification of the tale: Is it primarily about curiousity, particularly that of women, and its punishment? Or does it concern the envy of the gods over the favored position of Prometheus? Paul Schwarz, in *Die Neue Eva,* claims that the purpose of Hesiod's tale, from beginning to end, is simply to portray women as evil:

Pandora is created as an evil for men, and when the cursed woman opens the fateful jar, the envious and furious Zeus has finally reached his goal: the punishment of mankind. The anti-feminist epithet *"kalòn kakón"* (beautiful evil) demonstrates that Hesiod regards the evil of the world to be grounded in the existence and nature of women.[20]

✢

It is Hesiod's charming, malicious version of the myth of Pandora that has made its way into Western culture. Neither Roman religion nor the Latin poets showed much interest in the story, but because it was so widely known and provided pagans of the first and second centuries with an alternative myth of the creation of Woman, the early Church Fathers could hardly avoid confronting it. Origen (ca. 185-254), in refuting the Gnostic Celsus, defended the superiority of Genesis by simply quoting Hesiod's story at length, "fitted of itself to excite laughter." He chided "him who would give to these lines a grave allegorical meaning (whether any such meaning be contained in them or not)."[21] Tertullian (ca. 160-230) mentioned the story in an address to women in which he opposed the wearing of chaplets (flowered crowns). He too was affected by the charm of the story:

If ever there was a certain Pandora, whom Hesiod cites as the first woman, hers was the first head to be crowned by the graces with a diadem; for she received gifts from all and was hence called "Pandora"; to us, however, Moses . . . describes the first woman, Eve, as being more conveniently encircled with leaves about the middle than with flowers about the temple.[22]

Although Origen and Tertullian had every reason to deny outright the truth of the story, they equivocated, with statements such as "whether any such meaning be contained," and "if ever there was

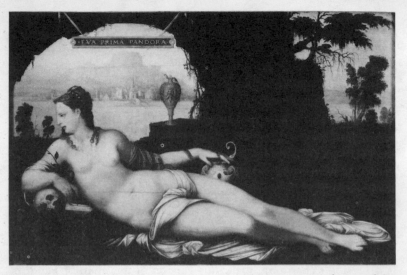

Eva Prima Pandora, by Jean Cousin; 1550. A clear artistic confusion of the Eve and Pandora stories. By permission of the Louvre, Paris; photograph by Musées Nationaux.

a certain Pandora"; it appears that the Church Fathers were unwilling to leave all the good stories for the devil! So, later, Gregory of Nazianzus (ca. 320-380) retold the story with noticeable relish before he dismissed it as a pagan fable. But then, returning to the biblical story of the Fall, he provided it with a markedly antifeminist moral. Hesiod had done his work on Gregory; henceforth he described Eve as "vain," "fraudulent," "immodest," "self-seeking," and "prurient."[23] John Chrysostom (ca. 347-407), clearly influenced by Hesiod's characterization of Pandora as a "beautiful evil," tried his own hand at oxymoron:

> What else is woman but a foe to friendship, an inescapable punishment, a necessary evil, a natural temptation, a desirable calamity, a domestic danger, a delectable detriment, an evil nature, painted with fair colors?[24]

It is clear that the Church Fathers did not dismiss the story of Pandora in favor of Scripture; instead they preserved it as a completion of, and commentary on, the story of Eve. The two accounts of the first woman became one. "The Fathers of the Church," write

Dora and Erwin Panofsky, "in an attempt to corroborate the doctrine of original sin by a classical parallel, yet to oppose Christian truth to pagan fable, likened Pandora to Eve, a step the full effect of which was not felt until the sixteenth and seventeenth centuries."[25] Erasmus later retold the story in what proved to be the definitive reading, in *Adagiorum Chiliades Tres.* In the version told by Erasmus, the container of evils (it was an error on the part of Erasmus that transformed *pithos* into *pyxis,* "box") is brought by Pandora into the house of Epimetheus, and it is clearly due to her "feminine traits" of curiosity, deceitfulness, impetuousness, and fatal beauty that she becomes the instrument of the downfall of the race.[26]

One final word must be spoken about Pandora. It appears that the myth played a fateful role in the negative sexualization of the story of the Fall during the postapostolic period of the Church. Theodore Reik notes that "intensive misogynist tendencies that dominated a certain late phase of Greek civilization transformed the lure of the female body into an organ of danger and terror and turned the sexual attraction of women into a malicious temptation."[27] The once holy body of the Mother Goddess, that *pithos* that contains all goods necessary for life and receives back the body born from it, became for Hesiod an object of horror, disgust, and fear. Because the Church Fathers found this idea congenial for their own purposes, it too was carried into the interpretation of the story of Eve. Pandora's story has survived the centuries. Reik reminds us that "the student of the symbolic language that pervades all primitive myths will easily guess that the vessel in which all evils are contained represents the female genital (compare the vulgar English expression "box" for vagina")[28]

Thus the symbol remains, and continues to do its damage. In Panofsky's *Pandora's Box* we are told that

Paul Klee, in a painting dated from about 1920, pictured the ominous receptacle as a kind of goblet containing some flowers, but emitting evil vapors from an opening clearly representing the female genital; and following World War II Max Beckmann painted "Pandora's Box" as a small, square object charged with an incalculable amount of energy and exploding into a chaos of shattered form and color as an atomic bomb. Thus Pandora, whom Voltaire called "the original sin," has served to symbolize the sin which may turn out to be our last.[29]

Pandora's Box as Still Life, by Paul Klee; 1920. Whereabouts unknown. Photograph by the Museum of Modern Art, New York.

3. The Lady of the Rib

There is something very strange and singular about the creation of Eve.[1]

In the panel depicting the Creation of Eve, which is located exactly at the center of the Sistine Chapel ceiling, God beckons Eve out of the side of the sleeping Adam. The interpretation of Genesis 2:22 is literal here. Eve's hands are folded prayerfully, her mouth half-open in surprise or awe. The thickness of her body suggests that she is to be the mother of all humanity, but no hint is given that she is destined to bring about the fall of her husband and all her progeny. Theologically and morally, Michelangelo's portrayal of Eve may be said to be neutrally correct.

But there are other Eves on the ceiling. In the more famous rendition of the creation of Adam, she appears unborn beneath the crook of God's left arm, her eyes fixed upon her husband-to-be as he receives the spark of life. She is Eve who is yet to come and, as we shall see, come again.[2] In a third panel she turns away from Adam to receive the forbidden fruit from the outstretched arm of a noticeably female snake. In another scene in the same panel she glares back unhappily at the angel who drives the guilty pair from paradise. Across the center of the ceiling, Leo Steinberg has shown, a diagonal "line of fate" that passes directly through the figures of Eve in the *Creation of Adam, Creation of Eve,* and *Temptation* panels may be drawn.[3] Artistically and theologically, then, Eve is seen by Michelangelo as the primary clue to the entire drama of birth, paradise, sin, and earthly existence. Eve's biblically correct introduction into the world, placed as it is at the exact center of the entire composition, is the real point of no return for humanity. Her appearance is its downfall, and not her disobedience in the garden.

Creation of Eve, by Wiligelmo; 1100–1106. Adam is noticeably pregnant. Duomo, Modena. Photograph by Alinari.

Creation of Eve, by Jacopo della Quercia; 1425-1438. San Petronio, Bologna. Photograph by Alinari.

✳

Michelangelo chose one of two Genesis accounts for his portrayal of Eve's creation. In the first chapter of Genesis, God creates
"mankind" in his image. As if to stress that the creation of "mankind" includes the female of the species, the writer repeats: "In the
image of God he created him, male and female he created them."
The direct consequence of creation in God's image is the governance of the earth and all its creatures; therefore the simultaneous
creation of the sexes is significant. If the woman is created at the
same time as the man, it follows that she shares equally in the work
of governance.

The contradictions between this story and the account of the
creation of the first human pair in Chapter 2 of Genesis have long
been troublesome to commentators. In the second story, God
forms *adam,* (a single, representative being) out of *adamah* (a clod
of earth) and animates him with the breath of life. Because God
determines that "it is not good for man to be alone," he creates
the animals and birds subsequent to the creation of the man, and
brings them to him to receive names. But among the creatures no
fitting helper *(ezer)* is found. God resolves to create such a being,
forms the first woman out of a rib of the sleeping man, and presents her to him. Adam accepts her happily and gives her the name
Woman *(ishshah,* said to mean "taken out of man," who is called
"*ish*").[4] The implication of the story is clear: Created after the
man, out of his substance and especially for him, her purposes are
subordinate to his.

Orthodox Jewish and Christian theology has always accepted the
second of the creation stories more comfortably. One reason for this
is doubtless because the rib story is the more charming. And taking
the Genesis 2 account literally can allow that charm to transfer itself
to the character of Eve. If she is part of Adam's body, she cannot be
regarded as alien to him.[5] She is, as Adam sings, bone of his bone,
and flesh of his flesh. It is impossible to miss the ecstasy in Adam's
outburst at the joyful shock of recognition: *"This* one at last!" The
most popular stories concerning the creation of Eve came to be those
concerning the union of the first pair, and the scene of the meeting

of Adam and Eve was transposed into the wedding that set the standard for all weddings.[6] God himself plaits the hair of Eve and adorns her with jewelry, and then, acting as best man for Adam, erects ten canopies for the couple. Attending angels serve as musicians, servants, and guests. Eve is an object of wonder and delight. Christian theology sometimes appears to have continued this rabbinical tradition; the New Testament united the themes of paradisiac companionship and domestic order in sermons on congregational unity and Christ's love for his Church-bride.[7] Thomas Aquinas drew the moral lesson that Eve is "taken from near to her husband's heart" so that he might "love woman all the more, and cleave to her more closely."[8] Augustine, in *City of God,* points to the rib tradition as the basis for what has come to be a classic Christian statement about marriage: "The fact that the woman was made for him out of his side is also an effective symbol of the conjugal love that should unite husband and wife."[9]

It is surprising to discover on further investigation that this line of thinking is not, in fact, typical of either Jewish or Christian development of the rib story. What we find instead is a virtually unrelieved tendency to see in the story a statement about Eve's subordinate status or flawed character, a prophecy of what is to come in the next chapter of Genesis. Perhaps the writer, traditionally known as the Yahwist for his preference for this name for God, had this in mind. Remembering that Adam will later give the woman the name Eve, ("the Mother of All the Living,") we learn that in Sumerian religion the cuneiform signs NIN.TI could be read as either "lady of life" (a title for a goddess) or "lady of the rib."[10] The author may very well know this and wish to reflect on the circumstances of Eve's creation with a pun that is reinforced by the wordplay possible with the Hebrew *tsela* ("rib," but also "stumbling").[11] This cleverness is not at all beyond the powers of the Yahwist, who places the occasion of Eve's receiving of her name immediately after the completion of her starring role in the drama of humanity's great misstep.

✳

Jewish legends about the story of the rib and the circumstances of the woman's birth from the side of Adam may be more humorous or mischievous than vicious, but they are nonetheless almost unrelievedly misogynist. Consider those in the *Genesis Midrash* (A.D. 600 to 1200).[12] Eve is not created until there is an express demand for her, records one rabbi, because "the Holy One . . . foresaw that he would bring charges against her." (XVII.4).[13] She is created during Adam's sleep because "the beginning of a man's downfall is sleep: being asleep, he does not engage in study and does no work" (XVII.5).[14] As soon as she is created, Satan is created as well (XVII.6). God "considered well from what part to create her":

I will not create her from his head, lest she be swellheaded; nor from the eye, lest she be a coquette; nor from the ear, lest she be an eavesdropper; nor from the mouth, lest she be prone to gossip; nor from the hand, lest she be light-fingered; nor from the heart, lest she be prone to jealousy; nor from the foot, lest she be a gadabout; but from the modest part of man, for even when he stands naked, that part is covered. Yet in spite of all this, *"But ye have set at nought all my counsel, and would none of my reproof."* (Prov. 1:25) I did not create her from the head, yet she is swell-headed . . . ; nor from the eye, yet she is a coquette . . . ; nor from the ear, yet she is an eavesdropper . . . ; nor from the heart, yet she is prone to jealousy . . . ; nor from the hand, yet she is light-fingered . . . ; nor from the foot, yet she is a gadabout (XVIII.2).

Indeed, even the fact that the woman was constructed from bone explains why she acts as she does. She needs perfume, because bones putrify (man, made of earth, does not). She has a shrill voice, because a bone dropped in a hot pot will make a crackling sound. She can never be appeased, because bone soaked in water will never be saturated (XVII.8). Rabbi Joshua of Siknin, to whom we owe these last elaborations, derives from Genesis other explanations for the condition of Woman. She goes with her head covered because "she is like one who has done wrong and is ashamed of people"; she precedes corpses at funerals because it was she who brought death into the world; she menstruates as a reminder that it was she who shed Adam's blood; she must separate out the *ḥallah* when she bakes because she corrupted Adam who was "the world's *ḥallah*"; and she

extinguishes the sabbath lights because "she extinguished the soul
of Adam" (XVII.8).

These comments are representative, and what is remarkable is that
the account of Eve's creation from Adam's side should have attracted
so much negative commentary about women. But probably we
should probe no deeper at just this place. The *Midrash* is a minimally
organized collection of *bon mots* that does not pretend to impart
deeper religious or psychological insight, although occasionally it
does. Its function is to tell "just so" stories, which provide origins
of customs, rationalizations for scriptural contradictions, and suc-
cinct homilies. The stories of Adam and Eve do not occupy for
Judaism the crucial position they occupy for Christianity.

✳

We have already noted that in favoring the second account of
Eve's creation over the first (which they did almost without exception), the early rabbis surmised that each version carried important
implications for the religious and social order. It the woman is
created simultaneous with the man, she is "perfect" also, and shares
equally in the work of lordship. If she is created after him, she is
somewhat less than perfect and belongs to the realm over which he
excercises lordship. In preferring the second account, then, interpreters prefer an Eve who is religiously, socially, politically, and
sexually under the control of her husband.

Returning to the prologue to the story of Eve's creation from
Adam's rib, we discover that its assertion of sexual power and social
control provides us with the most important clue to the nature of Eve
as the Yahwist understands it. Adam appears to lack nothing for his
happiness; it is God, not Adam, who determines that it is not good
for him to be alone. In an insightful comment developed by Philo
of Alexandria (ca. 20 B.C.–A.D. 50), Adam objects to the creation
of the woman:

> Woman becomes for him the beginning of a blameworthy life. For as long
> as he was by himself, as accorded with such solitude, he went on growing
> like to the world and like to God.[15]

Creation of Eve, by Michelangelo; 1511. Sistine Chapel ceiling, Vatican. Photograph by Alinari.

Creation of Eve, by Lorenzo Maitani; 1310–1330. Duomo, Orvieto. Photograph by Alinari.

Interpreters in the intervening centuries have provided us with the picture of Adam's dejected loneliness, but in fact the text itself does not suggest why it should be that the solitude of the first man is not good.

The woman is to be Adam's *ezer* ("helper" or "partner"). One Jewish legend that the Yahwist probably did not know, but which is quite in keeping with pre-Yahwist Mesapotamian traditions concerning primal humanity, interprets this in a sexual way, claiming that Adam copulated with all of the newly created animals only to find them unsatisfactory partners.[16] This legend is at first hearing simply offensive, and it is certain that the word *'ezer* need have no particular sexual connotation. But if we understand Eve's sexual role as did the classical Christian theologians, to propagate the species rather than gratify Adam's sexual desire, it is not so offensive to imagine the naming of the animals as a euphemism for sexual relations with them. The animals are "named," Eve is created and brought to Adam, and Eve is "named." We have explored the significance of Eve's names without yet considering the importance of the act of naming. Genesis sees naming as being placed under the control of the one who names,[17] perhaps as a euphemistic reenactment of a primitive sexual ritual of subjugation. It is therefore quite right (even without a ritual copulation interpretation of the action, but more profoundly true if one allows it) for a contemporary feminist to say of this passage:

It is necessary to grasp the fundamental fact that women have had the power of *naming* stolen from us. We have not been free to use our own power to name ourselves, the world, or God.[18]

In this view, the naming is a kind of rape. On accomplishing the sexual domination of his satisfactory partner, the first male gives her a name, which formalizes a reversal of the normal course of events. She is "woman," *ishshah,* "taken-out-of-man." She is born from him, not he from her.[19]

Certainly, given his theological predisposition, the Yahwist could hardly have had Eve precede Adam in the order of creation. Not only would this have asserted the importance of procreation, it would also have suggested sexual congress between Eve and God in order to create Adam. The earthly order is intended to recapitulate the heavenly state of affairs: one male God who is Lord of heaven and one male vice-regent who is lord of the created order. Eve must show deference to Adam as she shows deference to her Creator in the center panel of the Sistine Chapel ceiling, which depicts her creation. The suggestion that Eve's creation is deliberately placed as the last of God's acts because she is the crown of creation is wishful thinking. Given the other features of the story and the purpose of her creation, that notion is utterly impossible.[20] She belongs to the realm of the creatures over which Adam will exercise his lordship.

✴

It can be argued that there is a countertradition that depicts Eve as a flawless creation, the epitome of beauty, grace, intelligence, and spiritual strength. We have already mentioned the Jewish legends connected with the paradisiacal marriage, legends developed further by the early Christian. Consider the poet Dracontius, writing at the conclusion of the fifth century:

> She stood before him, uncovered by any veil
> Her snowy body naked like a nymph of the sea,
> The hair of her head unshorn, her cheeks were made lovely with a
> blush,
> And everything about her was beautiful: eyes, mouth, neck and hands,
> Even as the fingers of the Thunderer could make her.[21]

Lest we imagine that she is solely an object of physical desire, Milton's passage in *Paradise Lost* depicts her as a completely suitable intellectual, emotional and conversational partner for her husband, a true companion.

> when I approach
> Her loveliness, so absolute she seems
> And in herself complete, so well to know
> Her own, that what she wills to do or say
> Seems wisest, vertuousest, discreetest, best;
> All higher knowledge in her presence falls
> Degraded; Wisdom in discourse with her
> Looses discount'nanced, and like folly shewes;

Eve, by Albrecht Dürer;
1507. Pitti Gallery,
Florence. Photograph
by Alinari.

> Authority and Reason on her waite,
> As one intended first, not later made.[22]

Is there, then, an Eve who is fully Adam's equal; in every respect
as much God's image as Adam is? But hear Milton further:

> Nature . . . on her bestowed
> Too much of ornament, in outward show
> Elaborate, or inward less exact.
> For well I understand in the prime end
> Of nature her the inferior, in the mind
> And inward faculties, which most excel,
> In inward also her resembling less
> His image who made both, and less expressing

> The character of that dominion given
> O'er other creatures.[23]

Eve is less equal. At her creation, she seems to reflect less of the Creator. Adam is naturally her superior, and naturally as superior "makes use of his subjects for their own benefit and good. . . . For good order would have been wanting in the human family if some were not governed by others wiser than themselves. So by a kind of subjection woman is naturally subject to man, because in man the discretion of reason predominates."[24] This kind of argument has, of course, been used historically to justify racism and totalitarianism, as well as sexism. Aquinas (ca. 1225-1274), whose formulation it is, borrows an idea from Aristotle in his attempt to explain how it can be that woman, though created in the image of God, is not quite up to the standard of Adam:

> For the active power in the seed of the male tends to produce something like itself, perfect in masculinity; but the procreation of a female is the result either of the debility of the active power, of some unsuitability of the material, or of some change effected by external influences, like the south wind, for example, which is damp.[25]

What the rib story provides for the conception of Eve, and her history, is the locus for the notion that the first woman has an inherent imperfection that makes it inevitable that she will succumb to the importunities of the serpent. In Chapter 5 we will examine the variety of forms this supposed natural weakness assumes. Here we should simply note that just as with the story of Pandora, Eve's created assets are considered to be her liabilities. We have, after all, heard something like the tribute of Dracontius to Eve before: This is Hesiod's description of the newly completed Pandora, with the gods and goddesses standing awestruck before the splendor of the new creature. Is it not, after all, precisely the feminine in Pandora that constitutes the punishment? Milton, too can speak of his Eve as "sovereign mistress"; "sole wonder"; "fairest resemblance to thy maker fair"; "sovereign of creatures, universal dame"; "goddess humane"; "a goddess among gods, adored and served by angels numberless"—but this is all put into the mouth of the serpent as he discourses with her.[26] Eve's attributes serve but to set the stage for the fall that she will precipitate.

Both Milton and his contemporaries regarded Eve as prejudiced toward Satan's arguments, as partly fallen before she actually ate the forbidden fruit. Already preoccupied with herself to a dangerous degree, she was "influenced," "fired" by Satan's flattering terms of address . . . while his promise of divinity proved "an argument suitable to her humor."[27]

Certainly Eve is beautiful—a "beautiful evil." Indeed she is a delight—a "deadly delight." Her gifts are what enable her to be a snare to men. For Dracontius and Milton, as for Hesiod, every account of the loveliness, grace, intelligence, and perfection of the first woman serves but to set the stage for her undoing. That which makes her female is what will enable the serpent to bring her down, or enable her to induce a righteous man to join her in her sin. Adam will be "fondly overcome with Femal charm."[28]

✳

Until normative Judaism concentrated attention on the *yetzer-hara,* the evil impulse, as the central feature of the doctrine of sin, and for a long time afterward in Jewish mystical circles, a perfectionist view of Adam accompanied a tendency to stress and elaborate upon the special guilt of Eve. Without suggesting that Adam's glory and majesty were at the same time his downfall, the rabbis and Kabbalists described and meditated at some length on the grandeur of the first man. A case could be made that the legends of Lucifer and Samael, which add such color and an element of psychological shrewdness to Jewish tradition, arose because of a desire to protect Adam himself from any suggestion of imperfection, of an inherent flaw.[29] Given the presumed need for Jewish and Christian theology alike to present the wickedness of humanity as utterly inexcusable and the primal pair as thoroughly culpable, it is not surprising that Eve's culpability should have been of such interest. But Adam's was not; the tendency to deny his capacity for sin was accompanied by the ever more strident assertion that it was his partner who possessed some flaw in her character which would bring about the downfall of humanity.

Increasingly, it is assumed that Eve was created with a greater capacity to sin than Adam. She is, as Augustine might have put it, *non posse non peccare*—incapable of *not* sinning. Just as Pandora's vessel becomes one with her, Eve is regarded as forbidden fruit and as the serpent. She is sin awaiting its opportunity and it is in the Garden, just as in the house of Epimetheus, that she escapes the watchfulness of her husband and the opportunity is provided.

4. The Serpent-Mother

Eve is still in the present story halfway a snake; the snake
halfway a demon.[1]

What does an apologist for Judaism or Christianity do with the
discovery that there are two contrasting accounts of the creation of
the first woman? In the previous chapter we showed how the account
of Eve's creation from Adam's rib was the preferred of the two
stories, not only because of its charm and intimacy, but because of
what it suggests about Eve's status and character. But the account of
simultaneous creation in Genesis 1 is equally scriptural and could not
be ignored. How could the two be reconciled?

The most common resolution of the problem assumed that the
woman created from Adam's side was not the woman created in
Genesis 1. Commentators supposed that God had made one or more
attempts to provide Adam with a mate until he succeeded with Eve.
One such legend imagines that the earliest Eve was created out of
filth and sediment rather than the pure earth used for Adam, and
therefore had to be discarded.[2] Another pictures Adam awake during the creation of his consort-to-be, increasingly repelled by the
sight of the glands, hair, skin, and organs as they are assembled, and
unable to accept the finished product.[3] Finally, after putting Adam
to sleep God tries once more. He creates the woman out of a part
of the man so that he will not reject her. He presents her to Adam
only when she has been adorned with jewelry and her hair has been
carefully plaited.[4] Adam accepts her with ecstatic poetry:

> This one at last is bone of my bones,
> and flesh of my flesh!

The most famous and certainly the most profound of the legends
that tried to come to terms with the problem of the two creations

confronts the political and social implications of the stories directly.[5] It seems that the first woman, whose name was Lilith, never tired of reminding Adam that since she was created at the same time, it followed that she was of equal status and need accept no subservient role. The resulting quarrels came to a head when Adam insisted that the sexual act be consummated only in what has come to be called the missionary position. Lilith regarded the position as demeaning and refused; when Adam attempted to force her, she pronounced the divine name of God and fled to the shores of the Red Sea, there to realize her sexual fantasies with demons. Divine missions to secure her return to Eden were unsuccessful; she protested that her misadventures had, in any event, rendered her an unsuitable wife for Adam. Thus a new wife had to be created for Adam, one who would be clearly subordinate to him. Lilith, because she was not present in the Garden of Eden for the Fall and its penalties, did not die. She lives forever as a demonic, highly erotic night spirit who snatches newborn children (particularly males) and assaults the bodies and senses of men who sleep alone (presumably an explanation for erotic dreams).[6]

In time Lilith's story became confused with the story of Eve. In Canto XIX of the *Purgatorio,* for instance, Dante relates a dream-vision that comes to him at four o'clock in the morning, when the moon has ceased to cool the earth and the sun has not yet begun to warm it. He is confronted by "that ancient witch, for whose sole sake the mount above us [that is, the earthly Eden] weeps."[7] The witch is Lilith, fulfilling her ancient role of tormenting men in dreams. But she is also Eve, who forfeited paradise. Dante, like modern feminists, recognizes in the first witch the reverse side of the character of the first woman, her shadow role, the embodiment of that rebelliousness and assertiveness in women that men must hold in check.[8] Eve must be guarded constantly to ensure that she is an enabler rather than a disabler, the Mother of Life rather than a destroyer of life. The story of Lilith thus seems to embody the deepest male fears of impotence, weakness, and isolation in the face of unfettered female sexuality, assertiveness, and independence. Raphael Patai's *Hebrew Goddess* details the struggle of Judaism against such embodiments of female power down through the centuries; they include Lilith and Lillake, or Lillitu (the Canaanite wind spirit, from whose

Cylindrical vase with female deity; middle of the third century B.C. Iranian import into Mesopotamia. By permission of the British Museum, London.

⸓

name Lilith is possibly derived), Lamia, Astarte, and other pagan goddesses of the Near East who polluted pure Yahweh worship and time and again had to be driven from the temple.[9]

Immediately following the expulsion from the Garden, the creature Adam has named "woman" receives another name from him: Eve or ḥawwāh, said by him to mean "the Mother of all the Living." This verse has always presented special problems to biblical scholars, both because of its position in the story and the ambiguity of the name.[10] It seems to honor the woman, though that would be strange in view of what has just transpired, and it supposes that she has borne children, although at this point in the story she has not. The etymology proposed by the Yahwist—that is, the connecting of ḥawwāh with the Hebrew ḥay ("living")—is not persuasive. No consensus exists among scholars concerning the true meaning of the name.

But Bruce Vawter defends the placement of the verse in the text and poses an alternative suggestion for the name:

First of all, it has been placed as immediately as possible after the lines
that proclaim the woman's condition as one of subjection to her husband,
and namegiving is, as we know, the prerogative of one in dominance.
Secondly, there may be here another of those wordplays in which the
Yahwist took pleasure. . . . Not in the Hebrew preserved in the Bible but
in the cognate Arabic and Aramaic languages a word related to ḥawwāh
means "serpent" (in Aramaic, ḥiwya). This consonance has been pointed
out from the time of the earliest Jewish commentators on the text. Whatever
may once have been the sense of the ḥawwāh (serpent-mother = mother-
goddess?) which the Yahwist decided to read as "mother of all the living,"
. . . he may very well have recognized its etymological appropriateness for
the present context. What the woman is in her historical state, after all, for
good as well as for ill, she owes to the intervention of the serpent.[11]

The association between Eve and the serpent, and between the
serpent and Satan (the *Sammael* of Jewish legend and the *Shaitan* or
Iblis of the Qur'an) is made again and again in interpretations of the
story of the creation and fall of the first humans. It is not simply a
matter of relating the mysterious proto-Eve, Lilith, to the demonic
realm. Eve *herself* is explained in terms of that realm, not only to
account for her activity in the garden, but to describe her material
substance and to provide a motive for her creation. She is held to
be the devil's mouthpiece, Satan's familiar. At times she *herself* is
seen in some way to be the forbidden fruit, or the serpent in paradise, or even the Fall. It is this association between Eve and the
serpent that we will explore for the remainder of this chapter.

It is an interesting possibility that the long history of the connection between Eve and the serpent begins with the Yahwist himself
and the relationship, whether in derivation or in sound, between the
name ḥawwāh and the Aramaic and Arabic words for snake. Perhaps
the writer meant to recall that ancient association between sacred
women and serpents in religions of the Near East. Snakes were
thought to control "wisdom" (magic), immortality, and fertility. As
such they were the special companions of women, and often guarded
earthly or celestial gardens of delight.[12] At times they were embodiments of Woman, as in the case of *Tiamat*.[13] In any event, Eve's
future activities were read back into the account of her creation, into
the material of her body, and into the very reason for her being. Her
future association with the serpent in the Garden demonstrated

clearly enough for many interpreters that far from being created in the image of God, she shared her substance with some personification of evil.

⋆⟨

"The creation of woman," writes Paul Schwarz, "gave the folk tale many possibilities for the expression of misogynist thoughts and the motif of female guilt for the loss of the paradisiacal life."[14] It is indeed remarkable that it is Eve's creation, rather than her actions in the Garden, that are the occasion of this misogyny, and that this misogyny so often takes the form of relating the newly created woman to the serpent. Many of the stories collected by Schwarz simply ignore the Yahwist claim that Eve was created from the side of Adam and the Priestly writer's claim that she was created in the image of God, and instead connect her material substance to the serpent, or to Satan, or to an appendage associated with both—a tail. From Schwarz's study I will discuss a representative few.

Schwarz relates a Jewish legend that holds that it was really Adam's tail that provided the raw material of Eve, leaving man from that time on with a useless coccyx as a reminder. A Bulgarian story expands on this idea, relating how the devil's tail replaced a rib carried by an angel to God during Eve's creation[15], and there is a similar account in the writings of Hans Sachs, the great figure of early German literature:

> God put aside the rib of the dormant Adam and pasted the wound over with earth. While he washed the blood from his hands, a dog stole the rib. God then cut off the dog's tail, from which he formed Eve.[16]

In the same vein, a popular Islamic legend supposes that the woman and the serpent possess the same devilish substance, and another story solves two etiological problems with one stroke: Eve was created from the feet of the serpent; "That is why women are so false, and why since that time the serpent has no feet."[17]

Other stories stress motivation rather than material identity: It was God's intention that Eve would bear evil into the world. The interestamental *Secrets of Enoch,* which we will examine in this chapter, holds that "death should come to Adam by his wife" (xxx.18),[18]

Eve, by Henri Rousseau; after 1904. By permission of the Hamburger Kunsthalle, West Germany.

while Anglo-Saxon religious poetry speaks darkly of "the brew . . . which Eve prepared for Adam at the beginning of the world . . . later poured for Adam, her dear husband."[19] Ophite Gnosticism and Manichaeism, two early Christian heretical groups, regarded

Eve as infused with a demonic sensuality that Adam could not withstand: "(The Prince of Darkness and his companions) created Eve also after the like manner, imparting to her of their own lust, with a view to the deceiving of Adam."[20] This entire line of thinking is perhaps summed up in the contemptuous prayer of a Jewish mystic who reminds us that, after all, Eve was created as the last of the animals:

> Lord of the world! Thou hast created Adam with thine own hands and spoken to him face to face, then thou gavest him to a lecherous woman. If only lechery had come into the world through a person rather than an animal![21]

Certainly these writings must be regarded as heterodox or, at the least, typical of neither Judaism nor Christianity. But we cannot really understand the imaginations of more orthodox writers without establishing the "demon-Eve" tradition, and considering how tenaciously it gripped the imaginations of the shapers of Eve.

The serpent was regarded, consciously or unconsciously, as a powerful symbol for the connection between evil and sexuality. The original transgression was seen from a very early date as having something to do with sexual awareness. Eve thus becomes the vehicle for the intrusion of *lust* into the created order. Anatole France is said to have observed to a student that "one knew that there was a hell, but its geography was unknown until that violent African Church Father discovered its door at a certain place between the legs of women."[22] He was thinking, no doubt, of Tertullian and the notorious "Devil's gateway" remark which we will examine in the next chapter, but he might have said the same thing of Augustine who, in his development of the doctrine of the transmission of original sin focused on that same gateway "between feces and urine," that place to which the idle hand of Michelangelo's Eve points, Spenser's "darksome hole." From the genital of Woman all men have come forth, and to the genital of Woman most men return. Psychologically, then, women must be regarded as perpetually confronting men with the threat of nonexistence, and men avoid this terror by reversing the natural course women are really born from men) or by denying their sexual yearning for the comfort of oblivion (women are seducers).[23] Thus the association of the first woman with the devil-snake in legend and art ought not to surprise us. Eve must be the creation of Satan, or created by God out of Satan's substance, or placed on the earth to do Satan's bidding.

$$\asymp$$

How is it that the rib has been fleshed out in just this way? What is the history of the "demon-Eve" association? In the Yahwist's account, the serpent is identified neither with Satan nor sexuality, and certainly not with Eve. He is simply, for the sake of what will transpire, "shrewd."[24] We have been told that the man and the woman are created in the image of God, and in neither creation account is Eve's innocence prior to the Fall questioned. We are actually not given any motive at all for the transgression of the divine commandment, and although the "knowledge of good and evil" that changes forever the existential state of affairs can mean several things, it does not in itself point to sexual discovery as either the Fall or the result of the Fall. "The woman," Vawter writes with some impatience, "is not really portrayed by the Yahwist as a temptress who beguiles man into misdeeds. Genesis does not share in the motif common in ancient mythologies according to which a woman was the cause of the miseries of a disordered world ("Pandora's Box" is a familiar example)."[25] Where, then, did the demon-Eve solution to the question of evil originate?

Theodore Reik was not the first and is unlikely to be the last to maintain that it was the Christian Church Fathers who originated the reading of the Fall as a horror story about sexual awareness, brought about through the perfidy of the temptress, Eve.[26] But in fact, the theme was already prominent in Jewish writings prior to the writing of the New Testament. It was, rather, the Christian scheme of salvation outlined by Paul that led the Church Fathers to focus on a single event as the introduction of sin into the world. Jewish theologians had no such compelling need, and thus never required belief in a single, primal transgression or original sin that was somehow transmitted to all humanity. Genesis itself, after all, suggests other possible beginning points for sin, any one of which might have been developed into doctrine: the pollution of humanity by fallen divine beings (Gen. 6:1-8); the *yezer-ha-ra* ("evil impulse") planted at birth

—a primitive, destructive shadow self that each human being must master (Gen. 8:21); the tower of Babel story, with its moral about human pretensions to divine status (Gen. 11:1-9); and the description of sin as a crouching, predatory beast in the story of Abel's murder by Cain (Gen. 4:7).[27] Until the conclusion of the first century A.D., theological discussion concerning the true origin and nature of human sin was in fact fluid and lively, and only after some time did Judaism gradually settle for the *yezer-ha-ra,* while Christianity developed into dogma its single-minded fascination with the story of the Garden of Eden.

The first half of the intertestamental period was notably attentive to the problem of the origin of evil. Interest in the Watcher legend of Genesis 6:1-8 was particularly keen. In those verses the Watcher angels—*bene-ha elohim,* or "sons of God"—are infatuated with the "daughters of men" and invade the world to consort with them, producing polluted but heroic human children, "mighty men that were of old, the men of renown." This corruption of humanity convinces Yahweh to put an end to the whole of creation, and although from the story it is difficult to understand why humanity should be held to blame, this is offered by the Yahwist as the motive for the destruction of the world by the flood.

Neither the Watcher story nor the account of the incident in the Garden of Eden is mentioned elsewhere in the canonical Old Testament. But writings that became a part of the Apocrypha[28] show an obvious interest in the unique offspring of the human women and the "angels" (for so the monotheistic Jews came to regard the mysterious *bene-ha elohim*), attributing to them an unusual arrogance (Wisdom 14:6), rebelliousness (Sirach 16:7), or folly (Baruch 3:28). The most important and influential of the non-Apocryphal intertestamental writings, the *Apocalypse of Enoch* (second century B.C., also known as *Ethiopic Enoch* and *Enoch I*) recounts at length both the Garden of Eden story and the legend of the Watchers. The Garden of Eden is shown to Enoch in a vision, but no moral judgment is made concerning what is supposed to have happened there; it is simply the place where Adam and Eve acquired wisdom. The knowledge they obtained is not sexual or moral but technological—what we might call the arts of civilization. It is true that the imparting of this wisdom signals the close of the paradisiacal age, and in that sense it may be said to be evil, or at least make it possible for men and women to act wickedly. But *Enoch I* does not impute evil and wickedness to Adam and Eve because of any particular action on their part.

It is the elaboration in *Enoch I* of the Watcher story that marks the beginning of the demon-Eve solution to the problem of the origin of evil. This part of *Enoch I* is actually a fragment of an earlier work, probably called the *Book of Noah,* written prior to 161 B.C. and close to the spirit and theology of the *Book of Jubilees.* The leader of the rebel angels is one Sâmjâza, and the band numbers 200. They formally covenant, descend on Mt. Carmel, and then proceed to take wives from among the daughters of men. Significantly, it is the angels, and not the hapless women, who are defiled by the union: "They began to go into them and to defile themselves with them" (7:1-2). The women are taught "charms and enchantments, and the cutting of roots" and are "made acquainted with the wild plants," that is, they are given that special folk knowledge that in time comes to be associated with witches.

The Watchers then proceed to "devour mankind." They teach the arts of civilization to humans, each teaching his special technical skill. The connection is thus made once more between knowledge of a technical kind and moral degeneracy: The getting of wisdom goes hand in hand with wickedness. "There was much godlessness, and they committed fornication, and they were led astray, and became corrupt in all their ways" (8:2-3). Earth complains to heaven that "the children of men may not perish through the secret things that the Watchers had disclosed and taught their sons" (10:7-8).

Two literary confusions are at work here: technical knowledge is confused with sexual activity, and the rebelliousness of the Watchers is confused with the apparently innate seductiveness of human women. One Watcher, Gâdreêl, is singled out as the one who "led astray Eve" (69:6). But who is really the party guilty for the corruption of humanity? The writer seems to acknowledge that the reader will have some difficulty understanding why the willful actions of the angels should be held to the account of humans, so an explanation, conclusive but unpersuasive, is provided:

Two Watchers Descending to a Daughter of Man, by William
Blake; 1796. Rays of light emanate from the gigantic
phalluses of the Watchers. Rosenwald Collection, by permission of the National Gallery, Washington, D.C.

Angels Descending to the Daughters of Men, by John Flaxman; ca. 1821. By permission of the Fitzwilliam Museum, Cambridge, England.

Sin has not been put on the earth, but man of himself has created it.
. . . And barrenness has not been given to the woman, but *on account of the deeds of her own hands* she dies without children (98:4-5; author's italics).

The Apocryphal *Book of Sirach* (ca. 280 B.C., also called *Ecclesiasticus*) leaves even less room for ambiguity: "From a woman was the beginning of sin, and because of her we all die" (25:24). It is likely that *Sirach* reflects the tradition that it was Eve who first fell in the Garden of Eden, but the Watcher story provides further opportunity to affix the blame. *The Testament of Reuben* (from *The Testament of the Twelve Patriarchs,* ca. 109-106 B.C.) warns the reader to:

Pay no heed to the beauty of women, . . for evil are women, my children; and since they have no power or strength over man, they use wiles by outward attractions. . . . Women are overcome by the spirit of fornication more than men, and in their hearts they plot against men. . . . For a woman cannot force a man openly, but only by a harlot's bearing she beguiles him (4:1, 5:1-4).

Hesiod could not have said it better. And particularly noteworthy is the charge in *Reuben* that the daughters of men actively seduced the Watchers. The Watchers put on human disguises when they came to earth, and the women "lusted in their minds after the forms" (5:7).[29]

A full characterization of Eve appears in *The Books of Adam and Eve* (100 B.C.–A.D. 300), where there is also a good deal of commentary about the events in the Garden of Eden. Although this writing is composed of stories and traditions drawn from different sources and different centuries, its portrayal of the first woman is seamless. Eve is consistently complaining, self-pitying, wheedling, and pathetic. She considers herself fully to blame for the expulsion from the Garden ("On my account hast thou been driven hence" (3:1-3); "I have brought trouble and anguish upon thee" (5:3)). She seems to be incapable of penance; after asking Adam to teach her penance, she is seduced again by Satan (10:2-3). She tells Adam that by rights he should live and she should die because of her inability to remain faithful (18:1-2). Adam, on the other hand, is heroic and strong (6:1), able to secure forgiveness for her so that the race might be perpetuated (21:1-3). The soul of chivalry, he explains to Seth that he is partly to blame for the presence of pain in the world, since he too is guilty of the Fall (32:1ff.). But when Seth is bitten by a serpent, Eve denies that Adam was blameworthy. In a narrative that has come to be called *The Gospel of Eve*[30], she tells of her seduction by the serpent and the eating of a fruit poisoned by him, so that when she spoke to Adam it was with the voice of Satan.

The Book of the Secrets of Enoch (30 B.C.–70 A.D., also known as *Slavonic Enoch* or *Enoch II*) may represent the decisive stage in the fusion of the Watchers legend with Genesis 3. A fallen angel, here named Satona or Satomail and described as the leader of the Watchers (Chapter 18), functions as the serpent who "conceived thought against Adam [and] in such form . . . entered into and seduced Eve, but did not touch Adam" (31:6). This seduction account, which is Hellenistic in style and content, is juxtaposed with a passage fully in keeping with the more traditionally Palestinian style and content of *Jubilees* and *Sirach,* which describe Adam in the perfectionist terms that were to become increasingly popular in Judaism during the next several centuries, and which were to provide the basis for Paul's presentation of Christ as the second Adam.

How seriously did the Church Fathers take these writings? *Jubilees, Sirach, Wisdom,* and *Baruch* were widely regarded as authoritative in a church for which a canon of Scripture had not yet been established, and the latter three eventually entered into the Roman Catholic canon. The author of the New Testament Letter to Jude was not averse to quoting *Enoch* for support (Jude 14-15), and there can be no question of the familiarity of other intertestamental writings to early Christian theologians. Tertullian regarded *I Enoch* as authoritative, and it is to him (probably not coincidentally) that we owe the explanation of those New Testament passages requiring the veiling of women in church. Tertullian explained the custom as one meant to dissuade the angels from responding once more to the seductiveness of their bared tresses.[31]

Both *The Testament of Reuben* and *The Books of Adam and Eve* are Gnostic in spirit, and cannot be said to represent normative Jewish attitudes. But it should be remembered that at the time of their writing, there was no such thing as normative Judaism, let alone orthodoxy. The influence of such works on subsequent rabbinic Judaism has yet to be fully explored. Certainly Philo, to whom Jewish and Christian writers of the first several centuries are heavily indebted, shared much of the world view of the intertestamental writings, notably their misogynist outlook. Consider his discussion of the customs of the Essenes, that separatist and puritanical sect of Judaism contemporary with the intertestamental period and responsible for the Dead Sea scrolls. Before he has finished with his description of the outlook of the Essenes, there can be no doubt that we have entered into Philo's own mind:

No Essene takes a wife, because a wife is a selfish creature, excessively jealous and an adept in beguiling the morals of her husband and seducing him by her continued impostures. For by the fawning talk which she practices and the other ways in which she plays her part like an actress on the stage, she first ensnares the sight and hearing and then, when these victims have, as it were, been duped, she cajoles the sovereign mind. . . . For he who is either fast bound in the love-lures of his wife, or under the stress of nature makes his children his first care, ceases to be the same to others and unconsciously has become a different man and has passed from freedom to slavery.[32]

⊹

What we have in the various legends that relate Eve to the serpent, and in the story of Lilith, which provides Eve with a shadow side, is a reflection of the tendency within Judaism and Christianity and the cultures to which both have contributed to see Eve as demonically tainted from the moment of her creation. This tradition weaves together pagan associations of holy women with snakes, a special demonic sensuality supposedly inherent in women, and the suggestiveness of the biblical text that made such speculation possible, if not inevitable. Eve becomes the prototypical *femme fatale* long before she has her encounter in the Garden, just as Pandora is created to bring about evil.

Certainly the demon-Eve tradition does not appear in quite so crude a form in normative Jewish and Christian theology, and is, in fact, repudiated. But in the next chapters we will see how this tradition has nevertheless instructed orthodox views of Eve's character and the events in the Garden.

II. FALL

The LORD God planted a garden in Eden, in the east, and placed there the man whom he had formed. And from the ground the LORD God caused to grow every tree that was pleasing to the sight and good for food, with the tree of life in the middle of the garden, and the tree of knowledge of good and evil.

GEN. 2:8-9

The LORD God took the man and placed him in the garden of Eden, to till and to tend it. And the LORD God commanded the man, saying, "Of every tree of the garden you are free to eat; but as for the tree of knowledge of good and bad, you must not eat of it; for as soon as you eat of it, you shall die."

GEN. 2:15-17

The two of them were naked, the man and his wife, yet they felt no shame. Now the serpent was the shrewdest of all the wild beasts that the LORD God had made. He said to the woman, "Did God really say: You shall not eat of any tree of the garden?" The woman replied to the serpent, "We may eat of the fruit of the other trees of the garden. It is only about fruit of the tree in the middle of the garden that God said: 'You shall not eat of it or touch it, lest you die.' And the serpent said to the woman, "You are not going to die, but God knows that as soon as you eat of it, your eyes will be opened and you will be like divine beings who know good and bad." When the woman saw that the tree was good for eating and a delight to the eyes, and that the tree was desirable as a source of wisdom, she took of its fruit and ate. She also gave some to her husband, and he ate. Then the eyes of both of them were opened and they perceived that they were naked; and they sewed together fig leaves and made themselves loincloths.

Then they heard the sound of the LORD God moving about

in the garden at the breezy time of day; and the man and his
wife hid from the LORD God among the trees of the garden.
The LORD God called out to the man and said to him,
"Where are you?" He replied, "I heard the sound of you in
the garden, and I was afraid because I was naked, so I hid."
Then he asked, "Who told you that you were naked? Did you
eat of the tree from which I had forbidden you to eat?" The
man said, "The woman you put at my side—she gave me of
the tree, and I ate." And the LORD God said to the woman,
"What is this you have done!" The woman replied, "The
serpent duped me, and I ate."

GEN. 2:25-3:13

And to the woman he said,

> "I will make most severe
> Your pangs in childbearing;
> In pain shall you bear children.
> Yet your urge shall be for your husband,
> And he shall rule over you."

To Adam he said, "Because you did as your wife said and ate
of the tree about which I commanded you, 'You shall not eat
of it,'

> Cursed be the ground because of you;
> By toil shall you eat of it
> All the days of your life:
> Thorns and thistles shall it sprout for you.
> But your food shall be the grasses of the field;
> By the sweat of your brow
> Shall you get bread to eat,
> Until you return to the ground—
> For from it you were taken.
> For dust you are,
> And to dust you shall return."

GEN. 3:16-19

5. The Devil's Gateway

For though the devil tempted Eve to sin, yet Eve seduced Adam. And as the sin of Eve would not have brought death to our soul and body unless the sin had afterwards passed on to Adam, to which he was tempted by Eve, not by the devil, therefore she is more bitter than death.[1]

The first woman dominates the story of the Garden of Eden. It is Eve who converses with the serpent and who first violates the divine prohibition against eating fruit from the tree of knowledge. It is also she who then assumes the role of the serpent (we cannot tell whether Adam either knows or believes that she has had the encounter with the snake) in providing her husband with the fruit. Eve may be and has been portrayed as primarily guilty for setting in motion the series of events that end in the expulsion from paradise and the beginning for humanity of a state of existence characterized by pain, toil, alienation, and, at the end, death.

But is Eve primarily responsible for the fall? Contemporary interpreters of Genesis would have us believe that it matters little that it is Eve rather than Adam who plays the leading role in the story. Bruce Vawter calls to our attention the ancient literary convention that allowed only two characters to converse at any one time, suggests that with the serpent already on stage only one of the primal pair could make an entry, and claims that it is incidental that it should be Eve rather than Adam.[2] In any event, according to modern interpretation, Eve represents not her sex but the whole of humanity. Adam also falls, and with even less persuasion; it is humanity as a whole that must pay the penalty for having estranged itself from God. "In Adam's fall we sinned all"—what matter that Eve is the one who initiated the drama?

Relieving Eve of the special burden she has carried through 30

The bronze *Bernward Door;* ca. 1100. Hildesheim Cathedral, West Germany. Permission and photograph by J. Brüdern, Braunschweig, West Germany.

centuries of Jewish and Christian history has not impressed those who might be thought to most welcome it: contemporary feminists. Remarking that "the myth has projected a malignant image of the male-female relationship and the 'nature' of women that is still imbedded in the modern psyche," Mary Daly condemns contemporary attempts at "intellectualizing and generalizing the alleged content of the myth as a universal state of alienation."

Indeed this approach is intellectually bankrupt and demonic. It amounts merely to abandoning the use of explicitly sexist theological imagery while failing to acknowledge its still persistent impact upon society.[3]

The first thing to say about suggestions that we pay no particular attention to Eve's prominence in the third chapter of Genesis is that such an approach does violence to the story itself. A writer, after all, tells a story in his or her own way, and the duty of the reader is to respect the intentions of the writer and the integrity of the story. The second, and no less important, reason to reject the revisionist ap-

proach is theologically pragmatic. We can hardly come to terms with
the destructive patterns in our culture that the myth reflects and
supports, by ignoring, reinterpreting, or rewriting the ancient story.
For better or for worse, Genesis 3 is about a representative woman,
and not simply human nature. Through the crucial role she plays in
the drama, Eve's sin, and not just human sin, is thrown into high
relief. Because Adam and Eve are characterized as they are, human
history and social relationships are set in order in such a way that
certain possibilities are excluded.

Had Adam rather than Eve plucked the fruit, eaten, and then
encouraged his wife to do the same, we would have a very different
story from the one told by the Yahwist, and a doctrine of sin very
different from the one constructed by Christianity. The roles can no
more be reversed than Eve could have been created first and Adam
from her body, or Yahweh described in female rather than male
terms.

$$\star$$

Why Eve and not Adam? The Yahwist does not tell us directly just
why she engages the serpent in conversation, or why it should be the
woman who succumbs first to the tempter. But his interpreters have
been quick to fill the gaps in plot, motivation, and character, and are
nearly unanimous in supposing that she has this role because the
serpent, being shrewd, recognizes that she is the weaker of the two
humans. We have already discussed the opinion that while Adam
was created in the image of God, Eve represented a less than perfect
approximation of her Creator; inferior not only to him, but to Adam
as well.[4] She is a dilution in power, rational faculties, self-control,
piety, and moral strength. A flaw, present in her since her creation,
sets up the scene in the garden. "The pitiless devil foresees that the
man's brave heart may not be overcome by a serpent, so, under
cover of a pious voice, he approaches the ears of his wife." "Not
daring to accost the man because of his strength, he accosted as being
weaker the woman." "Satan first tried out his deceit upon the
woman, making his assault upon the weaker part of the human
alliance, that he might gradually gain the whole, and not supposing
that the man would readily give ear to him, or be deceived, but that

he might yield to the error of the woman." "Satan's cleverness is perceived also in this, that he attacks the weak part of human nature, Eve the woman, not Adam the man."[5] Several of the mystery plays went so far as to include a scene in which the serpent first approached Adam and was soundly repulsed. Luther was following a solidly established, if partially extrabiblical, tradition when he declared:

> Because Satan see that Adam is more excellent, he does not dare to assail him; for he fears that his attempt may turn out to be useless. And I, too, believe that if he had attempted Adam first, the victory would have been Adam's. He would have crushed the serpent with his foot and would have said: "Shut up! The Lord's command was different!"[6]

Paul's Letter to Timothy states it clearly and authoritatively for Christians: "Adam was not deceived, but the woman being deceived was in the transgression" (1 Tim 2:14). Adam was not taken in, because he was strong; Eve sinned because she was weak. It is in the attempt to define this weakness with more precision that Eve really receives her characterization at the hands of the shapers of the Eve tradition.

According to Schwarz's study, the dominant motive assigned to the Eve-Pandora character of those folk tales that concern the opening of forbidden boxes, jars, or bowls is curiosity.[7] This represents a relatively late diagnosis of woman's special weakness, however, and shows clearly how confusion of the story of the fall with the myth of Pandora influenced the interpretation of the biblical story in the Middle Ages. On the face of it, the charge that women are innately and fatally curious seems more mischievous than harsh. But Eric Auerbach, in his analysis of the twelfth-century Christmas play *Mystère d'Adam,* shows the true meaning of curiosity.

> There is no moral consciousness in her as there is in Adam; in its place she has a naive, childishly simple curiosity. . . . Eve has in no wise interpreted her conversation with the Devil as an experience of his treachery; her playful curiosity failed to grasp the ethical problem. . . . The Devil has shown her where her strength is greater than [Adam's]: In unconsidered action, in her lack of any innate moral sense, so that she transgresses the restriction with the foolhardiness of a child as soon as the man loses his hold upon her. There she stands, seductive, the apple in her hand, and plays with poor, confused, uprooted Adam.[8]

Curiosity is a frivolous amorality that the serpent persuades Eve to see as her real strength, rather than her weakness.

Or she is an easy mark because, unlike Adam, her insecurity renders her gullible. "The woman is less forseeing and sure of herself"; "in her doubt she could easily be persuaded into any opinion."9 This instability is linked with vanity. Augustine speaks of "a certain love of her own power and a certain proud self-presumption," and Aquinas agrees that she is "more puffed up than the man."10 This makes her an easy mark for the serpent, who has but to promise her a godliness that will befit her: "Such a destiny would well become your beautiful body and countenance, that you should be queen of the world."11 The Christian poet Avitus (beginning of the sixth century) imagines the Tempter's fulsome appeal:

> O happy one, ornament of the world, most beautiful maiden,
> Whom refulgent beauty adorns with blushing modesty:
> You are the future parent of the race;
>   the mighty world awaits you as its mother;
> You are the first and certain joy and comfort of man,
> Without whom he could not live.
>   Though he to whom you will bear children by your union
> Is greater than you, most gentle wife,
> He is subjected to your law by love.

Eve's ready response to the serpent's flattery testifies both to her gullibility and her vanity:

> As he promises such gifts with a fallacious whisper,
> The credulous woman marvels at him with a yielding look;
> And now she begins to hesitate more and more,
> and relax her feelings.12

The crowning achievement of this assessment of Eve's weakness is, of course, the famous introductory discourse of the serpent and the ensuring conversation with Eve in Book 8 of *Paradise Lost*. But Milton knew that what classical theology had called pride appeared in Eve's character as greed, and his poem portrays her thus. There is something in the Yahwist's understanding of the woman's mind that sounds startlingly like a principle of contemporary marketing and advertising: An attractive presentation will always take a woman's mind off the cost. She simply must have it. Dante had portrayed greed as the special motivation for the primal sin,13 and

Eve and the Future: The Serpent, by Max Klinger; 1880. By
permission of the Carus Gallery, New York.

Genesis itself states that Eve perceived the fruit to be "good for eating, and a delight to the eyes." Thus enticed, she takes it. Gerhard von Rad, whose modern commentary on Genesis insists that Eve bears no special guilt for the Fall, nonetheless explains her action by saying that "the woman confronts the obscure allurements . . . that beset our limited life more directly than the man does."[14] He should perhaps continue by saying that she confronts them more not because she has some innate drive to accumulate possessions, but because her social role is to do the shopping.

Others have identified the special susceptibility of Eve as her greater imagination. Cassuto, one of the more incisive of the modern commentators, notes that "in imagination the woman magnifies the effects of the eating amazingly; possibly for the very reason that a woman's imagination surpasses a man's, it was the woman who was enticed first."[15] But the real implications of this (unexamined) assumption are that she is attracted to the snake and the fruit because she lacks the moral discipline and reasoning skill to keep from being victimized by her senses. She has no intellect to hold her passions in check. She is the less rational, the more sensual of the pair.

It was Philo who developed this notion, and it became highly influential in both Judaism and Christianity: Man symbolizes mind, and woman symbolizes sense. It is Adam's recognition of the newly created Eve and his lapse into foolish poetry, that Philo sees as the real Fall. At that moment, sense triumphs over mind, the carnal over the spiritual.[16] In the struggle between humanity and the Devil, the woman is naturally more vulnerable because of her greater sensuality.

This is also the source of her hold over her husband, and the mystery of his inability to cope with her was resolved by placing her in league with Satan. She conspires against the man. She and the snake are in league by the time Adam eats the fruit; or, as Cassuto suggests, the cunning that the snake represents is really within Eve herself.[17] This is vividly depicted in Christian art; the serpent is often portrayed with a female head.

What is the basis for this convention? Probably the Yahwist's testimony that the snake originally did not crawl on its belly and that it was capable of human speech made possible the supposition that it had a human head. But Jewish tradition imagined the serpent as a masculine seducer.[18] At what point Christianity began to imagine a female snake is a matter of conjecture. The earliest translation of the Bible into Latin rendered the seducer as *serpens* (feminine gender), and that is possibly where the convention began. The earliest literary mention of the idea appears to be in the *Historia Libri Genesis* of Peter Comestor (d. 1173): "Satan chose a certain kind of serpent . . . having a virginal face, because like things applaud like."[19]

In an ingenious and influential essay, J. K. Bonnell maintains that the convention began with the mystery plays, which required long-haired actors for the role, because long hair was associated with divine beings.[20] Despite the fact that only males were on the stage in the Middle Ages, the snake came to be thought of as female, and was thus identified in the dialogue, beginning with the *Chester Play* in 1328 ("a mayden face, her kinde will I take"). Bonnell argues that the portrayal of the snake as a woman in painting (which began in the fifteenth century) followed the stage convention, rather than the biblical text.

The difficulty with this attractive thesis is that portrayal by painters of the snake as female actually predated the mystery plays, and the identification of women with snakes began, as we have already seen, centuries earlier. The mystery plays and the paintings that depicted the snake as female did, however, solidify the theory that Eve conspired with the Devil against Adam. In some of the many pictures of Eve conversing with her snake-woman adviser, one cannot escape the impression that the artist is governed by a male dread of conspiring females, the fear of the witches coven.

※

All of the supposed weaknesses of Eve—her curiosity, vanity, insecurity, gullibility, greed, and lack of moral strength and reasoning skill—combined with her supposed greater powers of imagination, sensuality, and conspiracy, are present in the sexual interpretation of the Fall, which sees the first transgression as human carnal activity. In this interpretation, the eating of the forbidden fruit becomes a euphemism for sexual congress between Eve and the snake, or between Eve and her husband; or the eating of the forbid-

Detail from *The Haywain*, triptych by Hieronymous Bosch, 1485–1490. By permission of the Prado, Madrid.

Detail from *The Terrestrial Paradise*, by the Limbourg Brothers, early fifteenth century. Illustration for *Très Riches Heures du Duc de Berry*. By permission of the Musée Condé, Chantilly; photograph by Giraudon, Paris.

Detail from *Adam and Eve*, altarpiece by Pseudo Met de Bles; first half of the sixteenth century. Pinacoteca, Bologna. Photograph by Alinari. Three paintings that show the serpent as Eve's double.

den fruit imparts to Eve a sexual consciousness that leads her to
seduce her husband. The idea of Eve as weak thus joins with the idea
that Eve is demonic: Having been seduced because of her weakness,
she is able to seduce her husband because she is filled with the power
of the Devil.

By the time of the beginnings of the Christian Church this picture
of Eve was already, as we have seen, an old story. The Watcher
stories established the beginning of corruption as the seduction of
heavenly beings by the daughters of men; women are depicted as
possessing a heightened sexuality that inevitably lures the sons of
God into the destruction of the paradisiacal state. Early Christian
theologians simply changed the actors in this tragedy from daughters
of men to Eve, and from sons of God to Adam, to produce a fateful
knowledge of the forbidden fruit and a consequent altered state of
humanity after the fruit is eaten. The original transgression is,
clearly, the introduction of sexual lust into the created order. Men
and women lose innocence and ever after must live in a world
dominated by *eros,* that demonic sensuality that alienates humanity
from Creator and man from woman. Eve is the diabolical vehicle for
this introduction, the special instrument of Satan's will.

The belief that the Fall was sexual in nature profoundly affects the
characterization of each of the participants in the story. The phallic
shape of the serpent establishes his purpose, turning him into an
irresistible suitor for the woman, calling forth from her the lust latent
in her since her creation. Conscious and unconscious eroticism in-
trudes into the most sober theological discussion of the significance
of the serpent. Satan "used the beast as a convenient organ for his
purpose, by means of which he might dangle the bait."[21] "He, that
evil charmer, framed his new device of sin against our race" by
dwelling "earthly and mundane as he was in will, in that creeping
thing."[22] Augustine holds that the serpent was deliberately chosen
because he was "slippery, moving in tortuous windings."[23] Thus it
becomes eminently clear why Eve, rather than Adam, should have
been the one to surrender to the serpent's urgings. One of many
Jewish stories concerning the encounter in the Garden claims that
what really happened is as follows: "In spite of all his urging [Eve]
remained steadfast and refused to touch the tree, then the serpent
engaged to pluck the fruit for her. Thereupon [she] opened the gate
of Paradise, and he slipped in."[24]

The Temptation, by Jacopo della Quercia; 1425–1438. Eve responds eroti-
cally to the serpent, while Adam reaches toward his genitals in sudden
awareness of his sexuality. S. Petronio, Bologna. Photograph by Alinari.

It is the special need of the Christian doctrine of sin that made this
interpretation of the original trangression particularly suitable. It is
held that the guilt of Adam and Eve is the guilt of all humanity, and
is thus an inherited guilt. Augustine asserted that the procreative act
passes on original sin; parents pass the sin on to children, eternally.

The fine point—that human sexual activity is not *itself* sinful, but passes on the sin—proved too fine. Intercourse itself became the sin. Sexual activity, that *eros* that could never be associated with the God of the Old Testament, became the characteristic mark of humanity's

Temptation of Eve, by William Blake; 1808. Illustration for Milton's *Paradise Lost.* By permission of the Boston Museum of Fine Arts.

sinful state of estrangement from its Creator, as well as the means whereby it continues to sin.

Eve's domination of the story suggests that she is the especially seducible one, and also that having been seduced by the wonderfully appropriate serpent/Satan, she then possesses a power over her husband that he cannot withstand. This explains *his* seduction. There is no more clear and bold a statement of this view than in the *Temptation* half of the *Temptation and Expulsion* panel of the *Adam and Eve* triptych on the ceiling of the Sistine Chapel. Eve is "seated with bent legs in a pose considered from antiquity as an erotic position, [her] voluptuous body outlined with rhythmic contours."[25] Her awkward position, when taken together with other features of the fresco, strongly suggests that she has just been interrupted at, or is about to engage in, oral copulation with her husband—a metaphorical eating of the forbidden fruit.

If we suppose that Michelangelo depicts Adam and Eve interrupted in sexual play at a moment preceding the Fall, we must of course assume their activity to be innocent. In that event, we could speculate that the artist stands within the tradition of that heretical notion which surfaced from time to time in Christian history and which was certainly prevalent (and persecuted) in the Bohemia of Michelangelo's time: that oral-genital, noncoital sex play was a feature of paradise. Certain libertine forms of second-century Gnosticism were accused of this by Christian apologists, and in the late fifteenth and early sixteenth centuries Roman authorities were fighting a particularly popular wave of it in Germany. Adherents imagined that the way to righteousness was to emulate the way of life of the primal couple, and therefore engaged in oral sex and public nudity. The sex play of Adam and Eve was seen as that of children: precoital, nonreproductive, virginal, and innocent. If we suppose that Michelangelo deliberately positions his Adam and Eve to suggest oral-genital activity, we could reasonably hypothesize that he knows of the so-called Adamite heresy.

But another fresco in the Sistina suggests that we are dealing with the depiction of the moment of the Fall itself. In the lower right-hand corner of *The Last Judgment,* painted decades later, there is little doubt that the Prince of Demons is being copulated by a snake.[26] The demonic figure and the snake comprise, as Steinberg has noted,

Adam, by Filippino Lippi; 1502. In the company of a small boy (probably Cain or Abel), Adam wearily contemplates his fate. Eve is present only in, or as, the serpent. Santa Maria Novella, Florence. Photograph by Alinari.

a union that portrays the concept of damnation itself. If Michelangelo intended for the *Temptation and Expulsion* panel to depict oral sexual activity, it is likely that he meant for it to depict the Fall itself.

In the same fresco Eve reaches toward the fruit with her left hand, at the urging of a female-torsoed snake. With her right hand, in an awkward gesture that can hardly be seen with the naked eye from the floor of the chapel, she points to her genitals. The two gestures are thematically related. "It is as if, upon the moment of grasping the apple, a spiralling force of cognition had raced through Eve's body, activating her idle hand to mime, in an almost reflexive way, the carnal consequence of her transgression."[27] But it is not an apple she receives; here, in keeping with Italian tradition, the forbidden fruit is a fig. The word *fico* would inevitably call to the mind of a sixteenth-century Italian the contemporary vulgarisms for the female genital (*fica*), as well as the contemptuous gesture made with the fist

Detail from *Temptation and Expulsion,* by Michelangelo; 1511. Eve reaches for the fig with her left hand and gestures suggestively with her right. Sistine Chapel ceiling, Vatican. Photograph by Alinari.

and thumb ("the fig") and the obscene term (*ficcare,* to "drive" or "thrust in") for sexual intercourse.

Adam, too, reaches for the tree. But he appears not to be reaching for the fruit so much as for leaves to hide his shame. When, in the other half of the panel, the pair is ordered out of the Garden, Adam's manner is little different from the representation of the scene by Masaccio, which Michelangelo used as inspiration: childishly terrified, penitent, but somehow resolute. But Michelangelo's Eve is more active and more adult. She turns her head in a gesture of dismay, but also with the sneering defiance of the Prince of Demons in the corner of *The Last Judgment.*

✳

"All witchcraft," we are told in the *Malleus Maleficarum,* "comes from carnal lust, which in women is insatiable. . . . Wherefore for the sake of fulfilling their lusts they consort even with devils."[28] This amazing document, recently reprinted and publicized by various feminist scholars, was, through 30 editions and 200 years following its publication in 1486, the most prominent, the most important, and the most authoritative treatment of the questions of how witches were to be explained, identified, accused, tried, tortured, and exterminated. Its clarity and persuasive argument, the integrity of its Dominican authors (one a Papal Nuncio and Inquisitor in Bohemia and Moravia and the other a future Dean of the Faculty of Theology at the University of Cologne), and the official approval given by the University of Cologne and Pope Innocent VIII, guaranteed that the work would be taken with the utmost seriousness by politicians, clerics, and legists who believed (as most did) in the terrible powers of witches, individually and collectively.

The *Malleus* bears a large share of the responsibility for the deaths of thousands of women at the hands of authorities, both secular and religious, Catholic and Protestant. Its arguments deserve the most careful scrutiny, particularly section I.6, which is entitled "Why it is that Women are Chiefly Addicted to Evil Superstition." The crudeness of the misogyny in this section of the *Malleus* is astonishing. "[Woman] is more carnal than a man, as is clear from her many carnal abominations." She is deceitful, with a "slippery tongue," "a liar by nature." She is naturally credulous and impressionable, therefore "quicker to waver in her faith, and consequently quicker to abjure the faith, which is the root of all witchcraft." Since women are "feebler both in mind and body," they have weak memories, are undisciplined, impulsive, and particularly dangerous when given authority over anything.[29] The authors' conclusion is a testimony to the strength and tenacity of the blending of the stories of Eve and Pandora: "Beautiful to look upon, contaminating to the touch, and deadly to keep"; "a wheedling and secret enemy."[30] The authors clearly have Eve in mind, an Eve responsible for carnal lust and death.

Three vices are especially characteristic of women: infidelity (in

Detail from *Temptation and Expulsion,* by
Michelangelo; 1511. Sistine Chapel ceiling, Vatican. Photograph by Alinari.

Expulsion from Paradise, by Masaccio; ca.
1425. Santa Maria Novella, Florence.
Photograph by Alinari.

both the religious and the secular sense), ambition, and lust. Among the peculiar marks of witches—women who manifest these vices to a higher degree and have methods to gain control over men—are a knowledge of contraception and abortion (a traditional domain of Lilith) and also power over male fertility and sexual performance. Males are immune to the direct stratagems of Satan chiefly because God chose to have a son rather than a daughter:

> Blessed be the Highest Who has so far preserved the male sex from so great a crime: for since He was willing to be born and to suffer for us, therefore He has granted to men this privilege.[31]

Witchcraft depends on a perverse political logic expressed in a less obviously perverse form by Milton in his depiction of the paradisical relationship between Adam, Eve, and God: "He for God only, she for God in him." The man alone may relate directly to God, and the woman's purpose is to work out her salvation by serving and loving the man. The *Malleus* sees Eve as specially related to Satan in a way Adam cannot be, capable of exercising a demonic power over her husband. Her special role in the Fall story, when combined with the mysteries of blood and sexuality associated with women, results in a prototypical woman who is for *Satan* only, and an Adam who must constantly guard himself against the Satan that is in her. Had Adam "eliminated" the woman (on Milton's terms by divorce,[32] on the terms of the *Malleus'* by actual execution) Satan would have had no power over him.

✕

Adam, of course, sins as well as Eve, but we are not told why he commits the sin. Commenting on Milton's *Paradise Lost,* Robert Lowell notes that the poet felt free to speculate at length on Eve's motivation for eating the fruit, but not Adam's.[33] An attentive Bible reader, Milton noted the peculiar fact that the Yahwist offers not the slightest clue why it is that Adam, apparently without resistance or conversation, takes the fruit from his fallen spouse and eats it. If the Yahwist cannot give us a reason, neither will Milton, and Lowell remarks on the consequent loss to the poem: The only interesting characters are Eve and Satan.

Cupid Complaining to Venus, by Lucas Cranach; 1529. In this confusion of traditions, Venus has assumed Eve's pose by the tree, wearing a hat of the artist's time. By permission of the National Gallery, London.

But where the Yahwist and Milton kept silent, others have had much to say. The stark biblical verse, "She also gave some to her husband, and he ate," leaves everything to the imagination, and 20 centuries of male rationalizing have indeed imagined just about everything to account for what must have transpired between Adam and his wife, and Adam and his own conscience. As perfectly strong as Adam is, he cannot withstand the onslaught of the now superhuman Eve. She makes use of her feminine powers and weaknesses alike to press her evil design: She lies, appeals to his marital faith, impugns his courage, whines, scolds, "moves his heart with a sudden sweetness," reasons, pleads, is sentimental.[34] And, of course, she is seductive:

But when Adam saw the beauty of the woman, she robbed the reason from his head. At the same time that she was stripped of the [paradisiacal] garments of light, her body shone like a pearl.[35]

"She robbed his reason": Left to his own devices, it is not conceivable that Adam would have sinned. He is a man without guile. It is Eve, not Adam, who needs to be watched. Cassuto recognizes what is suggested by the biblical text itself when Adam silently accepts the forbidden fruit from the hands of his wife:

In regard to the man, the Bible does not state his motives for eating, as it does in the case of the woman, since for him it suffices that *she* is the one who gives him the fruit. *It is the way of the world for the man to be easily swayed by the woman.* [36]

If it is the way of the world, it can hardly be Adam's fault.

"Active or passive," Schwarz writes, "the woman always tempts him to sin; she therefore bears the sole guilt for all the evil consequences."[37] Stoutheartedly, but in vain, Adam struggles against her. He holds out "according to some sages an entire hour, which is eighty years of earth time. . . . When he finally saw that Eve was still healthy and happy, he gave in to her and ate the second piece of fruit, which she had been offering to him three times a day."[38] This Islamic tradition owes much to similar Jewish stories, and in both cultures it was believed that wine played a decisive role.

In falling, "Adam was not deceived," according to Paul. Augustine took this to mean that although Adam had certainly sinned, he

Adam, Eve and Satan, by Michelangelo Naccherino; 1550–1622. Satan is depicted as half serpent, half pubescent girl. Boboli Gardens, Florence. Photograph by Alinari.

did so "with his eyes opened." Does this suggest perhaps a greater degree of culpability? It might seem so, but to Augustine, Adam yielded "by the drawings of kindred" because "he could not bear to be severed from his only companion, even though this involved a partnership in sin."[39] This heroic motive quickly established itself as the most satisfying. Adam was said to have sinned "out of a certain friendly good will, on account of which a man will sometimes offend God rather than make an enemy of his friends."[40] Adam sinned out of love rather than pride: "Fore lufe of hys wyfe" he gave up his inheritance; "fore Adam loued hyr and would not wroth her, he toke an appull"; "thus Adam for luf ete with dame Eve his wyue."[41] While Eve falls because of some feminine weakness or vice, Adam falls on account of his manly virtue. Unquestionably, hers is the greater guilt:

> By every garb of penitence [Woman] might the more fully expiate that which she derives from Eve—the ignominy, I mean, of the first sin, and the odium [attaching to her as the cause] of human perdition. . . . And do you not know that you are each an Eve? The sentence of God on this sex of yours lives in this age: the guilt of necessity must live too. You are the devil's gateway; you are the unsealer of that forbidden tree; you are the first deserter of the divine law; you are she who persuaded him whom the devil was not valiant enough to attack. You destroyed so easily God's image, man. On account of your desert—that is, death—even the Son of God had to die.[42]

Our sympathies are meant to lie with the hapless, well-meaning Adam who, much against his will, acts as a friend to his fallen companion and is "drawn by her into pestilent ambition."[43] That she was primarily at fault for the original crime was as clear to the older exegetes as it is to a contemporary psychoanalyst:

> Leaving God out of the discussion, as is seemly, we ask: What kind of a part does Eve play? If we can believe the story, she is the seducer. Without her that primal sin would never have been committed. Everything for Eve! Adam's fault was that he yielded to her. It seems that there is nothing left to his descendents but to regret his complacency.[44]

✧

When it came to reckoning the weight of guilt and apportioning the punishment for the transgression, the burden, of course, fell on

Eve. Peter Comestor's twelfth-century *Historia* was the first to relate Eve's greater punishment to her greater guilt: Since Adam only ate the forbidden fruit, he was sentenced to a reduced diet ("You shall eat bread," rather than every seeded plant as in Genesis 1:29). But Eve sinned twice—in pride and in disobedience—and was therefore punished twice. She is subjected to the rule of her husband, and complications will attend her own "bearing of fruit."[45] Vincent of Beauvais, early in the next century, discovered no less than four parts to Eve's sin, compared to two parts for Adam's: She coveted God's power, she disobeyed him, she persuaded Adam to join her, and she did not confess her guilt. Adam, on the other hand, merely ate the apple and attempted to pass on the blame.[46] And Thomas Aquinas held Eve's sin to be the more serious because she believed the words of the serpent while Adam did not, and because she made Adam sin as well. As for Adam: He joined her not out of malice but good will.[47] For her greater part in the crime, Eve is sentenced to sexual and domestic subjection to her husband, and the pain of childbirth. The meaning and significance of this sentence will be explored in the next chapter. But the biblical sentence is not the only burden Eve must bear. Her story, and the interpretations of her story, lay the major portion of guilt on her as well. She is destined to carry the blame for the alienated lot of humanity,[48] condemned to the end of her days to reflect on her greed, stupidity, amoral curiosity, willfulness, lack of sexual self-control, ambition, and cupidity. No more need be said than these words put into her mouth by a medieval Irish poet:

I am Eve, the wife of noble Adam; it was I who violated Jesus in the past; it was I who robbed my children of heaven; it is I by right who should have been crucified.

I had heaven at my command; evil the bad choice that shamed me; evil the punishment for my crime that has aged me; alas, my hand is not pure.

It was I who plucked the apple; it went past the narrow of my gullet; as long as they live in daylight women will not cease from folly on account of that. There would be no ice in any place; there would be no bright windy winter; there would be no hell, there would be no grief, there would be no terror but for me.[49]

6. "Mother Incest So Familiar to Us"

O certe necessarium Adae peccatum . . .
O felix culpa
(O verily necessary sin of Adam . . .
O happy fault)[1]

Beginning with the Enlightenment in the seventeenth and eighteenth centuries, the question was increasingly asked whether the story of the Fall might be better understood if it were freed from the fetters of dogma and religious tradition and approached simply as a human myth. As a universal rather than simply a religious story, might it not provide a clue to the very meaning of the word human, telling not of a Fall but rather a rise, a transition from infancy to adulthood, from blissful ignorance to risky but mature human knowledge, from animal instinct to human reason? Should we not, asked Schiller, see banishment from the Garden of Eden as "without doubt the greatest and most fortunate event in human history,"[2] as blessing rather than curse? And if the story were to be read in this way, would we not have to regard Eve as a female Prometheus rather than a Pandora, as a courageous benefactor who stole the greatest of gifts the deities were jealously withholding, rather than a villainess who had ended forever the state of universal bliss?

⸆

Those who regarded the story of the Fall as the great leap forward in the history of the race imagined that they were attacking the very enterprise of Christian theology, by translating the revelation of Christian faith into the terminology of human reason that was understandable and obtainable by all. But in fact, the notion of the *felix culpa,* the "fortunate Fall," is rooted deeply in traditional theological argument. The Christian story of salvation concludes, after all, with a victory; without an original defeat there can hardly be salvation, that amazing grace that conquers sin and death. If scholars writing during the time of the Enlightenment believed that without that transition narrated in mythical form in the story of the Fall there would be no human history or civilization, Christian theologians had long recognized that without the Fall there would be no sacred history, no *Heilsgeschichte,* because there would be nothing from which humanity could be saved. The fifteenth-century carol eloquently expresses the belief that, correctly understood, the Fall is not a misfortune but a blessing:

> Adam lay ybounden, bounden in a bond;
> Four thousand winter thought he not too long.
> And all was for an apple, an apple that he took,
> As clerkes finden written in their book.
> Ne had the apple taken been, the apple taken been,
> Ne had never our Lady abeen heavenè queen.
> Blessed be the time that apple taken was . . .
> Therefore we moun singen *Deo gracias!*[3]

That the scene in the garden might tell of a blessing rather than a curse was perfectly apparent to earlier readers of Scripture. Maimonides (1135–1204) recorded what was apparently a long-standing objection to Jewish belief: the absurdity that the consequences of disobedience should be "intellect, thought, and the capacity to distinguish between good and evil."[4] Centuries before, Gnostic writers were especially interested in what they regarded as a major flaw in the Christian doctrine of God. Surely knowledge is good, not evil? Then why not regard the serpent as a benefactor rather than a malefactor?

Since the creator god is not the true God at all, but a subsidiary and corrupt being, Adam and Eve's revolt against Yahweh takes on a reverse moral meaning. Rebellion against the creator becomes a virtue, and the serpent a benefactor of humanity who teaches us the principles of good and evil that the creator has been trying to hide from us.[5]

Of the Ophite Manichaeans, an early heretical sect, Irenaeus wrote (ca. 180) that "the serpent they magnify to such a degree that they prefer him even to Christ himself; for it was he, they say, who gave us the origin of good and evil."[6]

Celsus, the third-century Gnostic, made a distinction between a benevolent God who wishes only the best for his creation and who therefore would grant wisdom gladly, and the jealous God of the Old Testament (and of orthodox Christianity) who wishes to keep humanity enslaved. He believed that the biblical story of creation is nothing but a crude Jewish fable, and the allegorical explanations with which the Church Fathers sought to evade its absurdity were shameful. What kind of deity would wish to keep humanity in ignorance? One of the writings of the *Hermetica,* which championed the serpent's side of the conversation with Eve, can serve as a summary statement of the Gnostic attitude: "The vice of the soul is the lack of knowledge. . . . The virtue of the soul is knowledge. He who has got knowledge is good and pious; he is already divine."[7]

This line of argument led directly into the Enlightenment, centuries later. For Herder, Schiller, and Kant, the Fall represented a transition in human history that should be regarded as gain, not loss; through a spontaneous, courageous act humanity distinguished itself from the animals by choosing reason over instinct. Had this not occurred, the human being would "never have been released from the guardianship of the Natural; his actions would never have been free, therefore moral." Eden really represents "unconsciousness and servitude," for which humanity is "too noble."

As soon as his reason realized its initial powers, he spurned nature and her protective arms—or, better said: at the behest of an instinct which he himself did not even recognize, and unconscious of the greatness of the act he performed at that moment, he tore himself free from the benevolent ties which bound him, and with an as-yet-weak reason, accompanied only from afar by the instincts, flung himself into the wild play of life and set forth on the treacherous path to moral freedom.[8]

Schiller's words, with their high romance, sense of drama, and philosophical confidence in humanity's powers, are representative of the attitude of the Englightenment. Fundamentally, as a representative human being "Man" (seldom "Adam" and apparently never "Eve") perceives that the fruit of the tree is desirable as a source of wisdom, and that God must really intend for him to have it. In a brave, spontaneous, and profoundly human gesture he takes it, and with it the possibilities and consequences of a fully human existence.

It remained for liberal Protestant theology to provide the modern biblical underpinnings for the Enlightenment's analysis. Ninteenth-century biblical scholarship explained through the new critical science that earlier theological concentration on the evil consequences of the Fall story was mistaken. Good and evil must be understood, following the Hebrew original, to mean beneficial and harmful.[9] The knowledge obtained as a result of eating the forbidden fruit is knowledge in general, which makes Adam suitable for civilization:

An advance is now to be made: from a condition of mere innocence, which knows nothing else, man is to develop to one in which he himself freely decides for obedience to God and for that which is good. And, in so doing, he is to pass, not, indeed, through the antithesis of the good, i.e., guilt, but yet through knowledge of that antithesis. A knowledge therefore of the opposite of good must come and allure him. He must be tempted.[10]

For Julius Wellhausen, then, the narrative reflects a genuine advance in human development. Dillmann sees it as that point where humanity became capable of making ethical distinctions. The notion that the story has to do with an original sin is mistaken, a doctrinal consideration that has nothing to do with the author's actual intention. In any case, it can hardly be thought morally reprehensible for humanity to assume those powers that a more primitive consciousness would quite naturally describe to deity:

The first impulse to be awakened in mankind is envy of the prerogatives of the Lord. Why has he not bestowed upon his servant that life and knowledge which he keeps as his most precious possessions? Envy leads mankind to disobedience, and disobedience is followed by the loss of his place in Paradise. . . . The conflict between God and man is just as inevitable as that between master and servant.[11]

For those undaunted by the prospect of adjusting the traditional doctrine of God to suit the moral and rational advance of civilization, the Garden of Eden became understandable as a primitive myth about the dawn of human history, with psychological and sociological taboos described in religious terms and the violation of those taboos not only inevitable but beneficial.

※

In the late nineteenth and early twentieth centuries, anthropologists, ethnologists, and folklorists provided the research so that scholars of comparative religions could set the prehistory of Genesis

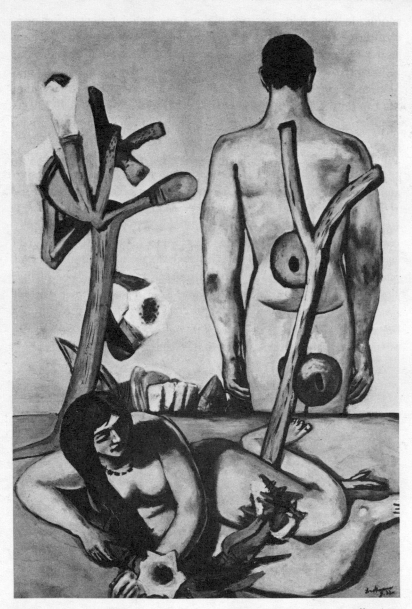

Adam and Eve, by Max Beckmann; 1932. By permission, private collection.

alongside tales that performed the same sacral function for non-Western or pre-Judaic cultures. Myths were myths, and if the contents of the stories differed, they could still be shown to have similar features by which they could be categorized. Thus organized, creation and Fall stories do indeed reveal features that are so constant we can only see them as, to use Joseph Campbell's phrase, "dialects of a single language." The following common tradition can be reconstructed: (1) Humans once enjoyed a paradisaical state of happiness with a deity or deities, free from work and the anxieties that now trouble human life; (2) collectively or individually, by design or default, humanity transgressed some limitation or divine prerogative; and (3) humanity was then cast into the state of toil, illness, and death in which it now lives.[12]

Certain motifs recur in the various expressions of this universal *ur*-myth (the original and fundamental story) often enough for us to reason that they cannot be coincidental: the eternal tree of life; the serpent who represents the demonic or guards what is forbidden, or both; a seduction; the enjoyment of a forbidden food or the refusal to eat a required food; and a perverted message or trick.[13] The suggestion, then, is that we should see Genesis as one version of a universal story, and thereby come to understand not only its meaning but the nature and function of myth itself. The underlying event in all of these stories may or may not be capable of reconstruction. Indeed, it is not an event at all in the usual sense of the word, but appears to have been a stage during which human beings entered into their own particular consciousness (or began civilization, or assumed a history), recorded in a variety of stories we call myths.

Scholars of the Enlightenment and nineteenth-century liberal Protestant biblical scholars largely ignored one feature of the Genesis story that had been decisively important to the Gnostics: the nature and function of the woman. But modern students of comparative mythology have found an almost universal misogyny in the creation and Fall stories of both highly developed and primitive cultures. Surveying the evidence, Schwarz remarks:

What these myths from high cultures have in common with the narratives from primitive cultures which we have previously sketched, and with the

biblical story with which we shall deal, is on the one side the loss of the
benefits of paradise, and on the other the connection of the calamity with
Woman.[14]

Schwarz finds it especially noticeable in African primitive myths of
origin that evil and death are laid to the account of women, "the
mystery of the Woman explaining the mystery of death." He records
a custom formerly observed by the male members of the Hanya tribe
of Angola, who beat their women whenever a death occurred, telling them, "You are the ones who brought death." He also provides
examples from South America ("The woman with her curiosity
spoiled everything"), New Guinea ("Women are seen to be responsible for the death sentence of mankind"), and China ("Woman is
the well-spring and root of all evil"). Remarking on the apparent
universality of the linking of women with evil and death, Schwarz
is reminded of Hesiod's Pandora, whose evils spread throughout the
whole world.[15]

✳

Twentieth-century interpretations of the Genesis story by comparative mythologists, folklorists, and psychoanalysts also restored that
feature of the myth that earlier theological commentators thought
most important and the Enlightenment and nineteenth-century biblical scholars had set aside: human sexual consciousness. The evidence
uncovered by the anthropologists and folklorists supports the contention that what transpired in the Garden of Eden was sexual discovery of some kind, in the course of which or as the result of which,
humanity entered into a new and alienating self-understanding. Eating magical fruits or foods reserved for the deities violated a taboo
because such fruit was the source of that divine wisdom that distinguished deities from humans. But such wisdom was fundamentally
sexual: The forbidden fruit was traditionally considered to have
aphrodisiac properties. The evidence collected by comparative religion and comparative mythology at this point is impressive, and we
need not stray far from Western culture or the soil of Judaism and
Christianity for examples of it. It was widely believed in the Middle
Ages that the unidentified fruit of Genesis 3 was an apple, probably

because the Latin *malus,* "apple," was the same word for "evil," but also because apples themselves had, at least since the time of the Hebrews and Greeks, sexual suggestiveness. *The Song of Songs* is but one work of literature that compares apples to female breasts. In ancient Greece and Rome, it was common to speak euphemistically of sexual activity as "stealing apples."[16]

Late nineteenth-century and early twentieth-century anthropologists and students of mythology and religion concentrated on particular features of the story, such as the serpent, the woman, or the fruit, but did not attempt a comprehensive answer to the wider questions. What was the relationship between misogyny and the origins of human consciousness or civilization? Why would the loss of sexual innocence and the acquisition of knowledge go hand in hand with guilt and alienation? Here the new science of psychoanalysis made the boldest and most original contribution to the history of the story of Eve, by building upon the findings of comparative mythology and structuring its evidence in accordance with psychoanalytic theory.

C. G. Jung and his followers understood Eve as one of a multitude of mythological representations of the Great Mother archetype. An archetype is a universal psychological symbol manifested throughout history in human dreams, art, images, and myths. The Great Mother archetype is—as are all archetypes—a union of opposites: "The Great Round that is primordial water, primordial parent, heaven, earth and underworld, merciful and avenging in one."[17] But what was experienced by preconscious humans as a unity becomes fragmented with the development of consciousness:

> This union of opposites in the primordial archetypes, its ambivalence, is characteristic of the original situation of the unconscious, which consciousness has not yet dissected into its antitheses. . . . As consciousness developed, the good goddess and the bad goddess . . . usually came to be worshiped as different beings.[18]

Thus the Great Mother archetype once combined angelic with demonic, comfort with terror, life with death. The development of consciousness, narrated in mythological form, reflects the rending of the unity of the primordial parent. Religiously considered, a meditation on creation will always be accompanied by the fear of regressing

Adam and Eve, by Hans Baldung Grien;
1511. Rosenwald Collection; by permission of the National Gallery of Art,
Washington, D.C.

Adam and Eve, by Max Beckmann, 1917.
By permission, private collection. Both
paintings illustrate confusion of the forbidden fruit with Eve's breast.

to the original chaos, of being destroyed by the goddess. Psychologically, the individual will always fear the return to the preconscious, to the womb of the mother, to death:

> For the ego and the male, the female is synonymous with the unconscious and the nonego, hence with darkness, nothingness, the void, the bottomless pit. Mother, womb, the pit and hell are all identical. The womb of the female is, as a womb, the womb of the Great Mother of all origination, the womb of the unconscious. She threatens the ego with the danger of self-naughting, of self-loss—in other words, with death and castration.[19]

We owe the development of this theory to Jung's disciple, Erich Neumann. Jung himself had little to say about the Garden of Eden story; his encounter with Genesis came late in his career, during his fascination with alchemy, and his own theories are consequently highly scholarly, mystical, elusive, and at any rate useless for our purposes. His early colleague and later rival Freud was likewise curiously silent about the biblical tale. When he developed a theory of an original crime—the killing of the father by the primal horde —the story of Moses was his biblical touchstone.[20]

Classical Freudian psychoanalytic theory sees the Mother Goddess as a projected image of the human mother. She is characterized in a paradoxical fashion because her image is formed by her offspring during its infancy, when the human mother represents all that is outside of the child itself. In the Oedipal situation, the male child must deny its father a role in procreation and reject the sexual nature of the mother; therefore the Mother Goddess is imagined as virginal. But as the child develops, this fiction cannot be maintained and is replaced by another: The now "traitorous" mother is regarded as a whore. The often destructive characterizations of goddesses are explained by this, as well as by the weaning process, which gives rise to infantile fantasies of consumption of the mother; this hostility is defensively transformed into an imagined consumption of the child by the mother.

Interestingly, it is in a letter to Jung (dated December 17, 1911) that Freud finally confronts the Garden of Eden story.[21] He warns against the "obvious" interpretation of myth (that which relies on the "surface version") and provides us in passing with his own partial analysis of the story. He champions Otto Rank's suggestion

Parua na te Varua Ino ("Words of the Evil Spirit"), by Paul Gauguin; 1892. Gauguin painted several female figures in this pose, including a monotype in which the demonic figure that appears here has been replaced with a snake. The cloth that she holds at her *pudenda* indicates the onset of menstruation. By permission of the National Gallery of Art, Washington, D.C.

in an article that the truth of the Garden of Eden myth is to be found not in its manifest but in its latent content. Rank holds that the myth deliberately and defensively "reverses" itself at several points, among them Eve's creation from Adam and her seduction of him. In reality, Rank argues, the opposite is the case: Adam is created from Eve, the primal mother. Adam seduces Eve. And it is God, not Satan, who converses with her in the form of the snake. Like any analysand, the Yahwist has distorted and disguised what he dare not admit. Freud concludes that what the story really tells concerns "the mother incest so familiar to us, the punishment and so on."

Subsequent psychoanalytic interpretation has concentrated on and developed this feature, reuniting it with that aspect of the story that was so attractive to the Enlightenment and nineteenth-century biblical scholars: The eating of the fruit is symbolic of humanity's attainment of knowledge, and thus its suitability for civilization. Something sexual *is* taking place, and something having to do with the beginning of human civilization is *also* taking place, and the one is the means by which the other is to be understood.

However obscure or excessive the findings of the psychoanalysts may seem, their interpretation of the story is complete and comprehensive; the first since Augustine. The clearest and boldest approach is Geza Roheim's study.[22] He draws heavily on the work of comparative mythologists, concluding that the crime is not only sexual but incestuous: "The fate of the woman is to give birth and therefore we expect the story to deal with coitus";[23] the punishment is, after all, suitable only for a sexual offense. As evidence that Eve is really Adam's mother, Roheim offers as proof not only Rank's thesis that the manifest content of the myth has reversed the latent content, but Adam's own words in Genesis 2:20. If Eve is "the mother of all the living," she must be Adam's mother as well. What has occurred in the story of the Fall is an aggression against God the Father: sexual reunification with the mother, Eve. Adam has committed incest.

That the punishment places the serpent and the woman in enmity with one another is also instructive. The serpent is clearly phallic, and if the punishment places the woman in opposition to the serpent, she is in opposition to the phallus. The earth is Mother Earth, and when the serpent is condemned to crawl on his belly on the earth, he is condemned to intercourse. The serpent and Adam must relate to the earth by crawling and plowing. Perhaps because he suspects that at this point he is stretching his evidence, Roheim supports his argument that the Fall is a sexual event by turning to comparative mythology for help, particularly the essay by Ludwig Levy, which sees in "eating" a euphemism for sexual activity, and the "fruit" as the female breast.[24]

In the psychosexual interpretation, a "crime" is also its own punishment. When one engages in sex, according to Roheim, it is actually always the mother with whom one has intercourse, always the father who is thereby sinned against. "The myth therefore simply tells us that sexual desire or maturation is disobedience to the father (Oedipus) and therefore a sin from the point of view of the invisible 'voice,' that is, of the introjected father-imago or Superego."[25]

The punishment of the woman is to give birth, but this is given short shrift because Adam is the hero in this interpretation, Adam who has transgressed against the father as the cost of his adventure. Sex, birth, and death are simply different parts of the same cycle. Adam must "till the soil," that is, he must return sexually again and again to the woman. Here he experiences the trauma of separation, the little death that follows orgasm, the separation from the mother that is always presupposed in his return to her, constantly renewed in sexual activity. In the language of the story, he is expelled from the garden, an image of birth that is also an image of death and separation. And expulsion from the garden also means that he must work, that is, work at civilization:

> The punishment suffered by Adam clearly shows that this change consists in growing up and even a superficial analysis of the myth shows that sexual maturity is regarded as a misfortune, as something that has robbed mankind of infantile happiness. . . . A bliss once enjoyed is now marred by anxiety, maturation is not a simple biological process but a misfortune. . . . It is hard to endure change. Separation from the Garden of Pleasure must be followed by aggregation to a new mother symbol, to the cultivated soil.[26]

Clearly, the sexual theory underlying the psychoanalytic theory of civilization has the profoundest implications for the understanding of Eve, and we shall return to this shortly in the final section of this chapter. At this point, however, we must gather up the various strands of evidence from the Enlightenment, from nineteenth-century higher criticism of the Bible, and from the findings of comparative mythology and comparative religion. In Erich Fromm's summation:

Adam and Eve at the beginning of their evolution are bound to blood and soil; they are still "blind." But "their eyes are opened" after they acquire the knowledge of good and evil. With this knowledge the original harmony with nature is broken. Man begins the process of individuation and cuts his ties with nature. In fact, he and nature becomes enemies, not to be reconciled until man has become fully human. With this first step of severing the ties between man and nature, history—and alienation—begins. As we have seen, this is not the story of the "fall" of man but of his awakening, and thus, of the beginning of his rise.

With Adam's "fall," human history began. The original, preindividualist harmony between man and nature, and between man and woman, was replaced by conflict and struggle. Man suffers from this loss of oneness. He is alone and separated from his fellow man, and from nature. His most passionate striving is to return to the world of union which was his home before he "disobeyed." His desire is to give up reason, self-awareness, choice, responsibility, and to return to the womb, to Mother Earth, to the darkness where the light of conscience and knowledge does not yet shine. He wants to escape from his newly gained freedom and to lose the very awareness which makes him human.

But he cannot go back. The acts of disobedience, the knowledge of good and evil, self-awareness, are irreversible. There is no way to turn back.

Man . . . can solve this dichotomy only by going forward. Man has to experience himself as a stranger in the world, estranged from himself and from nature, in order to be able to become one again with himself, with his fellow man, and with nature, on a higher level. . . . Man creates himself in the historical process which began with the first act of freedom—the freedom to disobey—to say "no."[27]

Taken out of Roheim's language of sexuality, the story told by the Yahwist is the story of the beginnings of human consciousness, human history, human civilization (Fromm's "higher level" at which humanity once more becomes one). The Fall is not a curse, but a blessing. It is the story of humanity becoming human.

⁂

Adam and Eve, by Hans Baldung Grien;
1519. Rosenwald Collection; by permission
of the National Gallery of Art, Washington,
D.C.

Criticism of the psychoanalytic interpretation of the story of Eve should focus on how well, or how badly, it explains her. She is depicted by Rank, Roheim, and Freud as the object and symbol of Adam's forbidden longing for a return to paradise, Mother, infancy, the womb. But his longing is ambivalent: To return is to forfeit independent life; to undo birth is to die. Thus Adam desires her and hates her at the same time. The latent message of the myth is that Adam, through his rivalry with his father, is the seducer of his mother. But because Adam cannot really desire an incestuous reunion with her, the death that return to her represents, she must be seducer as well as seduced.

The character of the woman and Adam's ambivalent attitude toward her constitute the real problem with the psychoanalytic interpretation of the myth. Roheim gives only the slightest hint that he recognizes an inner confusion in his theory when he states that "the enmity between the serpent and the seed of the woman means . . . the serpent (phallus) versus the female."[28] The psychoanalytic theory posits a struggle between son and father, but does not explain how this aggression becomes deflected toward the mother-wife as the one who has caused his birth or separation. Carried to the conclusion that Roheim does not develop, what he has outlined is not a theory of incest, but a theory of rape. Adam's destiny is to desire and despise, possess and reject women; Eve's, in the Freudian dispensation, is apparently to submit to that perpetual struggle for supremacy between male generations in which she is the perpetual victim.

Any literary study of the myth must reaffirm what the Gnostics believed to be true and comparative mythology rediscovered: The story focuses on Eve, not Adam. But the psychoanalysts, like Christian scholars, insist that it is Adam's story. It is about Adam's struggle with the Father-God, Adam's reunification with his mother, Adam's "aggregation to a new mother symbol, the cultivated soil" of civilization. Eve's part in this drama is reduced to that of a supporting actress by the technique of reversing the manifest content in which she has a starring role. She is now a function of Adam's maturation. Since the story is "really" about Oedipal behavior, it has to do with Adam's aggression toward his father and his illicit desire for his father's property—his mother—and not, as the Yahwist would have it, with Eve's own struggle.

Breton Eve, by Paul Gauguin; 1889. Eve's pose was suggested by a Peruvian mummy on exhibit at a Paris museum. At its first showing, Gauguin captioned the painting in the pidgin French used by prostitutes: "Don't listen to the liar." Bequest of Marion Koogler McNay; by permission of the Marion Koogler McNay Art Institute, San Antonio, Texas.

What, we must ask, can this "mother incest so familiar to us" mean for Eve? How can *her* psychology be understood by Roheim's claim that it is always the mother with whom one has intercourse? With whom is she struggling to reunite? Without a penis, and thus unable to "till the soil," what is her role in the creation of civilization? What sense can be made of her punishment if she has not, in the psychoanalytic reading of the story, committed any crime? These questions are not answerable, of course. Only the male matters here; Eve is but the prize in a male contest.

Psychoanalytic theory thus flows back into the mainstream interpretation of the story of Eve in the Western tradition, helping us to understand what it considers inevitable: what Lederer calls "the fear of women," and what Andrea Dworkin calls "woman hating."[29] In the attack of the sons of God on the daughters of men, it is the victim daughters that are seen as the corrupters and the aggressing males as the corrupted. The aggression that logically would be directed toward the Father God is deflected to the woman, where it assumes a destructive sexual form. The birth she gives is seen as a death; her presence is the permanent reminder of paradise lost. From the male point of view, sexual intercourse with her will always entail contempt and violence, and those words in the languages of the Western world that describe the closest intimacy between man and woman reflect that contempt and violence: hitting, driving into, poking, thrusting, and beating. The psychoanalytic interpretation of the story of Eve may provide us with a means of understanding this deflected aggression, but its vision, limited to the intolerable condition of male existence, can only provide us with a love that hates, and a longing that despises.

III. EXPIATION

But I am afraid that as the serpent deceived Eve by his cunning, your thoughts will be led astray from a sincere and pure devotion to Christ.

2 COR. 11:3

For a man ought not to cover his head, since he is the image and glory of God; but woman is the glory of man. (For man was not made from woman, but woman from man. Neither was man created for woman, but woman for man.) That is why a woman ought to have a veil on her head, because of the angels.

1 COR. 11:7–9:10

Let a woman learn in silence with all submissiveness. I permit no woman to teach or to have authority over men; she is to keep silent. For Adam was formed first, then Eve; and Adam was not deceived, but the woman was deceived and became a transgressor. Yet woman will be saved through bearing children, if she continues in faith and love and holiness, with modesty.

1 TIM. 2:11–15

7. "A Nail Driven into the Wall"

The essential point is that woman must always and in all circumstances be woman; that she must see and conduct herself as such and not as a man.[1]

Returning to what they regarded to be the certain Word of the Scriptures themselves, rejecting the sexual tendentiousness surrounding the fall of humanity as so much Jewish fable and Popish nonsense, the great reformers ordered a new trial for the first woman. Martin Luther (1483–1546) and John Calvin (1509–1564), authors of new commentaries on Genesis, dismissed fanciful solutions to the problem of the discrepancy between the creation stories; prior to the Fall, Eve is the equal of Adam, not simply as a bedfellow to the man, but as a life companion. "Eve was . . . in no respects inferior to her husband." "Eve was not like the woman of today; her state was far better and more excellent, and she was in no respect inferior to Adam, whether you count the qualities of body or those of mind."[2] Thus according to Luther, and hardly equivocal. Calvin's enthusiasm is only slightly less, and if he hedges on the issue of Eve's complete equality, it is only because of his vision of the moral perfection of the whole of creation. "It cannot be denied but that the woman was created after the image of God, though in the second degree."[3] We cannot be certain what is meant by "the second degree"; what is clear is that the manner of her creation does not suggest subordination. She is a companionable creature as like Adam as possible, in order to preclude "mutual contempt, . . . envie, . . . willes and contentions."[4]

Along with allegorical and speculative interpretation of Scripture. Calvin and Luther swept away such misogynist interpretation as Eve's supposedly greater sexuality, her greater culpability, and the belief that her offense was the direct result of some innate feminine character flaw. They rejected the Roman definition of the primal sin as pride. No, the Fall was first of all the Fall of the human pair together, and secondly, it occurred through their disbelief. Adam and Eve disobeyed God's clear command because they did not believe him. They were unfaithful.

This fresh approach could have provided a wholly new assessment of the story, one that would remove from Eve the onus of having

Detail from the *Sarcophagus of Junius Bassus;* fourth century. Vatican Museum. Photograph by Alinari.

been the one primarily guilty for bringing perdition to the whole
human race, and one that would reassess the harsh penalty that
followed from her crime. In fact, it did not. The reason is contained
in the double meaning of the word unfaithful. The infidelity of
Adam and Eve was not simply a lack of faith in God, but the rejection
of a sociotheological order of life established by God, the proper
observance of which required the acceptance of a structure of relationships among husband, wife, their work, and God. Although
Adam and Eve are of equal status in Eden, they must play carefully
prescribed and quite different roles. Adam's life project is the tending of the garden God has planted for him, Eve's is the tending of
her relationship with her husband: "The man should have respect
unto God, and the woman should be a helper of him thereunto."⁵
Her relationship to God is thus indirect, and dependent on Adam's.

For Protestantism, the answer to the question of who Adam and
Eve are is undercut by the domestic politics of paradise. God has
ordained a special political structure for Eden. In the great Puritan
epic *Paradise Lost,* Adam is answerable to God, Eve to Adam: "He
for God only, she for God in him."⁶ When Eve correctly understands her proper place in that divine-human order that is the true
paradise, she says:

> Unargu'd I obey; so God ordains.
> God is thy law, thou mine: to know no more
> Is womans happiest knowledge and her praise.⁷

But Eve, and then Adam, are unfaithful to that divine-human
order. Milton prepares us for the confrontation between Eve and the
serpent with a domestic quarrel; Eve suggests an equal division of
labor, and Adam responds that "nothing lovelier can be found in
woman, than to studie household good."⁸ Against Adam's objection
that it is his duty to guard her from all danger, Eve goes off by herself
—an echo of the story of Pandora—and it is when she is alone that
the Tempter finds her. Later, the newly fallen Eve meditates over
what has occurred and how she can talk Adam into sharing her sin:

> But to Adam in what sort
> Shall I appear? Shall I to him make known
> As yet my change, and give him to partake

> Full happiness with me, or rather not,
> But keep the odds of knowledge in my power
> Without copartner? So to add what wants
> In Femal sex, the more to draw his love
> And render me more equal, and perhaps
> A thing not undesireable, sometime
> Superior; for inferior who is free?[9]

This is an astonishingly modern outlook. In the words of Milton critic J. M. Evans, the Fall actually occurs when "for the first time in the poem she consciously stands on her own dignity." She responds to the urgings of the serpent because "after her quarrel with Adam she is in just the right frame of mind to listen sympathetically to tributes to her own dignity."[10] As Northrup Frye continues the argument: "What he says thereby instills in her the notion of her own individuality, somebody in her own right, herself and not merely an appendage to Adam or to God."[11]

By attempting to stand on her own before God, without at the same time standing before her husband, Eve fundamentally violates God's domestic arrangement. Central to this domestic arrangement is the married estate. Luther and Calvin firmly reject the belief that virginity and celibacy represent higher callings. Rather, it is not good for man or woman to be alone; alone they cannot be completely man or woman. Eve's crime, therefore, is in abandoning "the interdependence of true love for the independence of a dangerous adventure."[12] Despite the sexually suggestive language of the serpent in Book XI of *Paradise Lost* and the as-yet-unfallen Adam's description of her as "deflowered"[13] when she has sinned but he has not, her unfaithfulness to her husband and to God really involves her independence.

At the same time, Milton follows Church tradition in pointing to Adam as the one who is primarily to blame even though Eve must bear the greater burden of guilt. Eve charges Adam with failure to fulfill his duty toward her:

> Being as I am, why didst not thou the Head
> Command me absolutely not to go?[14]

Adam, in condemning her, admits as much:

Adam and Eve, by Lucas Cranach; 1526. Lee Collection; by permission of the Courtauld Institute, London.

> Thus it shall befall
> Him who to worth in woman overtrusting
> Lets her will rule[15]

Milton is expressing poetically a very Protestant point of view, which he elaborates in prose in his treatise on divorce. Adam would not have fallen if, at that point when she had invited him to join her in her sin, he had divorced her. What he is primarily guilty of is "excessive uxoriousness."[16] Calvin's verdict on the original sin is the same as Milton's: It is really Adam's fault because "Adam, who was set above the woman, yielded consent."[17] He is persuaded by Eve that he cannot deny her but must join her whatever the cost. Thus, in an act that Milton would have us believe is tragically heroic, Adam risks damnation out of love for his wife.

Paradise Lost thus arrives at the same conclusion reached by the rabbis centuries before in the story of Lilith: An independent woman can only represent a fundamental disruption of a divinely ordered state of affairs. Eve is said to be equal, but religious doctrine places her under Adam's control. To question this arrangement is to be unfaithful.

Returning, then, to our initial optimism concerning the views of the reformers on the subject of Eve's equal stature at creation, we see that we have not yet had Luther and Calvin confront those equally scriptural words that subordinate women to their husbands in the drama of salvation. The married estate in the New Testament is not only a social but a theological order. The reformers must receive their Genesis through the Letter to the Ephesians, where it states that wives must be "subjected in everything to their husbands." Eve's sentence is supposedly mitigated in the Christian scheme by subsuming it within the paradisaical marriage. Through subjection to Christ, and through the love of the husband she serves, Eve may at least ease her condition. The estate of Christian marriage must be, however imperfect, an approximation of Eden before the Fall. Thus, reading backward from the scene in the Garden to her creation, Luther must reconsider Eve's "equality": "She was, nevertheless, a woman. For as the sun is more excellent than the moon, so the woman, although she was a most beautiful work of God, was nonetheless not the equal of the male in glory and prestige."

"Nonetheless, Adam had some advantage over Eve. Just as in the rest of nature, the strength of the male surpasses that of the other sex, so also in the perfect nature the male somewhat excelled the female. . . . She is dependent on her husband."[18] One can almost hear the sigh of relief when Luther can at last describe the state of woman in marriage in a fallen world, where "the management of the household must have the ministration of the dear ladies":

Now there is added to these sorrows of gestation and birth that Eve has been placed under the power of the husband. . . .

This punishment, too, springs from original sin; and the woman bears it just as unwillingly as she bears those pains and inconveniences that have been placed upon her flesh. The rule remains with the husband, and the wife is compelled to obey him by God's command. He rules the home and the state, wages wars, defends his possessions, tills the soil, builds, plants, etc. The woman, on the other hand, is like a nail driven into the wall. She sits at home. . . . Just as the snail carries its household with it, so the wife should stay at home and look after the affairs of the household, as one who has been deprived of the ability of administering those affairs that are outside and concern the state. She does not go beyond her most personal duties. . . .

Women are generally disinclined to put up with this burden, and they naturally seek to gain what they have lost through sin. If they are unable to do more, they at least indicate their impatience through grumbling. However, they cannot perform the functions of men: teach, rule, etc. In procreation and in feeding and nurturing their offspring they are masters. In this way Eve is punished; but, as I said at the beginning, it is a gladsome punishment if you consider the hope of eternal life and the honor of motherhood which have been left her.[19]

Eve's sin is to have refused to be content with the "mutual love, delight, help and society of husband and wife, with the husband having greater authority."[20] For this refusal, she is sentenced to a more stringent version of the very role she has challenged. In his treatment of marriage in his *Christian Doctrine,* Milton follows closely the reformers' interpretation of the judgment, "Your urge shall be for your husband, and he shall rule over you." And Calvin's legal pronouncement arrives at the same point as Luther's homily:

For this speache, "Thy lust shall belong to thy husband" is as much in effecte, as if he should denied that shee should be free, on her owne, but subject to the rule of her husband, to depend upon his will and pleasure:

As if he should say, Thou shalt desire nothing but what the husband will.
Evenso the woman whiche had perversely exceeded her boundes, is restrained and bridled.[21]

Where earlier exegetes had held that one or another of Eve's
womanly traits latent in her since creation had led to the Fall of
humanity, the Protestant exegetes blamed her for leaving the watch-
ful eye of her husband, and him for allowing her to do it. She is a
failure as a helpmeet. And this view, after all, does not move the
reformers much beyond Gregory of Nazianzus:

> She indeed who was given to Adam as a helpmeet for him, because it was
> not good for man to be alone, instead of an assistant became an enemy, and
> instead of a yokefellow, an opponent, and beguiling the man by means of
> pleasure, estranged him through the tree of knowledge from the tree of
> life.[22]

And so the sin of pride becomes the sin of infidelity. What Protestant
analysis first denies or denigrates becomes the central feature, the
incarnation, of this doctrine. Eve's womanly unfaithfulness is the
other side of Adam's dereliction of masculine duty: Relinquishing
for a moment his sacred charge to restrain and bridle his wife, he
is—to use the rejected sexual language—cuckolded by the Devil.
Thus is the requirement of New Testament theology met: The Old
Adam must be found to be at fault so that Jesus Christ, the New
Adam, can redeem. But the real blame, and the unrelieved guilt,
falls on Eve.

⁂

For a modern Protestant consideration of Eve's nature and destiny
we can hardly do better than to examine the work of Karl Barth,
Calvin's greatest student and most persuasive apologist. Barth's sys-
tematic development of a doctrine of woman is consistent, subtle,
formidable, and—to his many feminist opponents—exasperating.
The large amount of space devoted to the subject in the pages of the
Church Dogmatics is indicative of the seriousness with which Barth
takes it, and in view of the vigor with which he argues that his
development of his doctrine is central to the understanding of the
whole subject of Christian ethics, we should not dismiss his argu-

Adam and Eve, by Rembrandt; 1638. Rosenwald Collection; by permission of the National Gallery of Art, Washington, D.C.

ment as quickly as his opponents have done thus far. Even when the *Church Dogmatics* fails in its attempt to soften Calvin's rigidity with a Mozartian celebration of the delights of *Mann und Weib,* Barth's straightforward engagement with the troublesome Old and New Testament texts pushes Scripture as far as it can go toward a positive picture of Eve. What, then, is Woman that Barth is so mindful of her?

Barth attempts to recapture the freshness and pastoral concern with which Calvin and Luther engaged the misogyny of medieval Catholicism with the weapons of *sola scriptura,* the Word alone, while avoiding the rigid view of domesticity that so restricts women in classical Protestantism. He begins by choosing his *scriptura* with shrewdness and imagination. Setting aside the Fall story itself as an account of the alienation of humanity that has nothing special to say about Eve, he concentrates instead on the creation texts of Genesis 1:26–28 and 2:18–23. At the outset he declares that this section of the *Church Dogmatics* will not be an *excursus:* The doctrine of woman is founded on creation in the image of God and this, in turn, is central to an understanding of God.

Barth's God is not solitary; it is his very essence to be in relation. The creation of humanity in the image of God means that humanity, too, exists only in relation. The image of God is an *analogia relationis;* like God, humanity is characterized in its essence by "relationality," by what Barth calls its *Mitmenschlichkeit,* or cohumanity:

> Could anything be more obvious than to conclude from this clear indication that the image and likeness of his being created by God signifies existence in confrontation, i.e., in this confrontation, in the juxtaposition and the conjunction of man and man?
>
> God created man in the basic form of all association and fellowship which is the essence of humanity.
>
> In isolation man . . . would not have been the being with whom God later willed to enter into relationship. . . . Solitary man would not be created in the image of God, who is himself not solitary.[23]

What does it mean to say that God is essentially in relation? This notion is critical for Barth's entire conception of revelation: Humanity is that race that is privy to the process by which God reveals himself to himself. In a clever sidestepping of the traditional literalbiblicist explanation of the troublesome divine plurals ("Let us make man," "Behold, the man has become as one of us") as a use of royal language or an anachronistic use of the doctrine of the Trinity, Barth imagines that God really is addressing himself. Such divine pauses to reflect occur only when humanity is created male and female in Chapter 1, and when the woman is created in Chapter 2. Barth believes this to be significant; just as the creation of the human pair results from God's reflective and covenantal character, cohumanity is the definition of human nature.

Cohumanity means not man with man, but man with woman. Man and woman must each address another being who is similar, yet dissimilar—a genuine "other."

In obedience to the divine command there is no such thing as a self-contained and self-sufficient male life or female life. In obedience to the divine command, the life of man is ordered, related and directed to that of the woman, and that of the woman to the man.[24]

It is not good for man to be alone; creation is not complete until Adam is no longer solitary, but truly man because he is man with woman. Eve is created as his flesh and blood counterpart, his 'ezer or "partner" (which Barth prefers to "helpmeet"), whom Adam recognizes, chooses, and confirms. Barth cannot overstate the importance of this event to the whole enterprise of creation:

The completion of all creation described here, i.e., the completion of man by the creation of woman, is not only one secret but *the* secret, the heart of all the secrets of God the Creator. *The whole inner basis of creation, God's whole covenant with man, which will later be established, realized and fulfilled historically, is prefigured in this event, in the mystery of man's emergence by the coming of woman to man.*[25]

Because his understanding of woman is based on God's creation rather than humanity's fall, Barth can make what appear to be utterly unambiguous statements about the full equality of women:

Man and woman are fully equal before God and therefore as man and therefore in respect of the meaning and determination, the imperilling, but also the promise, of their human existence. . . . They stand or fall together. They become and are free or unfree together. They are claimed and sanctified by the command of God together, and at the same time, with equal seriousness, by the same grace, to the same obedience and the reception of the same benefits.[26]

There is little in this of what has been called "the triumph of patriarchalism."[27] If Barth has placed more weight on heterosexuality than it can or ought to bear, nevertheless we have thus far in his theology a solid foundation for feminist theology. Phyllis Trible, using the same texts, arrives at the same conclusion: that 'ezer is a term of honor and dignity rather than reproach, and Eve's position as the last of God's creations shows that she is its completion and crown, not the Creator's afterthought.[28] But Barth, like Calvin and Luther before him, is now bound to reconcile equality before God and before Adam with the theological and social order established in Eden and reaffirmed in the letters of Paul in the New Testament. "Full equality" before God must now come up against the further witness of the Old and New Testaments, and Barth must necessarily speak of role, order, and place.

The New Testament makes it clear, if we should have any doubt, that Eve's creation as Adam's 'ezer subordinates her to him. "[Man's] strength and precedent are the reality without which she could not be woman."

The point of the name given by the saga is that woman is of man. This does not mean . . . that she is man's property. Nor does it mean that unlike him she is not a human being in the full sense. What it does mean is that in her being and existence she belongs to him; that she is ordained to be his helpmeet; that without detriment to her independence she is the part of him which was lost and is found again.[29]

Is belonging to man in being and existence really without detriment to her independence? Is she really a human being in the full sense? Again and again Barth claims that this is so, and he attempts to avoid the language of subordination and superordination in his discussion. In a passage overlooked by his critics, he even refuses to define the nature of male and female:

We have no right, especially if we ask concerning the command of God, to define or describe this differentiation. . . . The command of God will find man and woman as what they are in themselves. It will disclose to them the male and female being to which they will have to remain faithful. . . . In all this it may perhaps coincide at various points with what we may think we

The Fall, by Mabuse (Jan Gossaert); after 1510. Crossed arms and legs were artistic conventions for depicting sexual involvement. Detail from the Malvagna Triptych, Musio, Palermo, Sicily. Photograph by Alinari.

know concerning the differentiation of male and female. But it may not always do this. It may manifest the distinction in new and surprising ways. The summons to both man and woman to be true to themselves may take completely unforeseen forms from right outside the systems in which we like to think.[30]

But it appears that for Barth these distinctions cannot be demonstrated in ways that are *too* surprising:

The command of the Lord does not put anyone, man or woman, in a humiliating, dishonorable or unworthy position. It puts both man and woman in their proper place. Interpretations may vary as to where this place is, for the Lord is a living Lord and his mind is ever new . . . The essential point is that woman must always and in all circumstances be woman; that she must see and conduct herself as such and not as a man.[31]

The man must therefore, "in humility," assume a position toward the woman of "preceding her, taking the lead as the inspirer, leader and initiator in their common being and action." She must recognize that "in order she is woman, and therefore B, and therefore behind and subordinate to man. . . . Properly speaking, the business of woman, her task and function, is to actualize the fellowship in which man [as A] can only precede her, stimulating, leading and inspiring."[32]

There is no possibility in Karl Barth's theology that the full life of faith can be lived by men or women apart from their mutual interaction. For men to attempt to realize such a life with men, or women with women, is a most fundamental perversion. Barth's attitude toward homosexuality is that it is a terrible spiritual and physical sickness, to be understood and treated, but never to be accepted as a genuine possibility for the Christian life. Nor can the life of faith be realized by women who attempt to discover and stand upon their own individual integrity. Woman does not have "even a single possibility apart from being man's helpmeet. . . . Being herself the completion of man's humanity, she has no need of a further completion of her own."[33]

If she may and must lead her life as a woman, she too must consider that she has to render an account to man as he must render an account to her, that she is measured by his norms as he by hers. For this reason all the movements of man and woman in which there is an open or secret attempt to escape the reciprocal responsibility are suspect at least from the very outset. On both sides, everything is at stake here. . . . For both, therefore, there is only an incidental, external, provisional and transient isolation and autonomy. . . . Their being is always and in all circumstances a being with the other.[34]

There does, of course, exist the possibility of a disrupted relationship, and therefore of divorce. But so important is God's command and so clear are its implications that in most cases it is better for the woman to suffer at the hands of a tyrannical husband than to risk insubordination:

Even then it is better that she on her side should not infringe [on the marriage vow] but observe it. If there is a way of bringing man to repentance, it is the way of the woman who refuses to let herself be corrupted and made disobedient by his disobedience, but who in spite of his disobedience maintains her place in the order all the more firmly.[35]

To use a phrase that Barth uses often in his criticism of others: What are we to say to this? First, that he has provided us with the most attentive biblical understanding of the theology of the man-woman relationship that we are likely to have from Protestant scholarship. His attempts, however, to derive from the biblical text a defense of the independence and self-sufficiency of women through a self-consciously egalitarian scriptural analysis do not provide a persuasive alternative to what appear to be the clear intentions of the Old and New Testament passages. Barth has pushed and ordered Scripture as far as can be done toward a positive, affirming understanding of the nature and destiny of Woman; if he were to be challenged, it would have to be on a ground other than that his doctrine is "unbiblical." Nevertheless, Barth's arguments are clearly and completely unacceptable to his feminist critics.

To challenge Barth's position, we should begin with the often-quoted criticism of the *Church Dogmatics* as a whole, which at least here is quite appropriate: This is a theology for angels, not human beings. To argue that God's image is manifested in the creation of humanity as male and female in relation, and then to point to human sexuality as the mysterious heart of that relationship, is to require that sexual relations be full of *agape* (spontaneous, altruistic love), when often enough sexual relations do not even have adequate *eros* to fuel them. Would it not be more fruitful for Christian theology to reject once and for all the religious mystification and sanctification of sexuality, and focus instead on a Christological code of ethics that could speak to the myriad ways that men and women delight, console, instruct, and strengthen one another? And would it not then follow that it is completely possible for men to function as the other for men, and for women to do the same for women, thus giving theological structure and purpose to what Barth, with his strict heterosexual constraints, can view only with horror? Why could the relationship between men and women not realize itself in any or all of the other, nonsexual aspects of human relationships? To fail at heterosexual relationships or to succeed at homosexual relationships can only mean, according to Barth, that one has no theological foundation for one's faith. What has Barth's theology to say to that long and productive tradition in Western religion which validates, and even encourages, a decision for a solitary life? Jesus himself, as Muslim theology has long pointed out, lacked familial fulfillment, making necessary a final *rasul*—Muhammad the husband and *pater-familias*—who would provide a proper model for life "in relation." Surely the proper attitude toward this is to refuse to theologize about sex and agree that while the Christian life of faith must certainly be directed toward a community, the form and content of that community and the nature of one's relationship to it cannot be prescribed.

Also, we should question Barth's point of departure for his doctrine of Woman. The reformers found it necessary to develop their understanding of marriage along Pauline lines, accepting the Apostle's particular analysis of the Genesis story and his subsequent comparison of the relationship of husband and wife to that of Christ and the Church. Barth attempts to circumvent the problems resulting from such dependence on Paul by providing his own analysis of Genesis, founding his doctrine of Woman on the account of creation rather than the Fall, and thus on a relationship within God. But in doing so, he must suggest what his theology elsewhere would immediately proscribe, an idea that is foreign to the theology of the Old Testament—namely, that God is bisexual. This clever (and perhaps disingenuous) use of the notion of the divine *aseitas*—God's dynamic internal relationship—surely provides more aid and comfort to Jungian analysts and students of comparative religion than

Barth could ever wish. The notion is simply inconsistent with his most characteristic defense of the oneness, integrity, and majesty of a God who has nothing to do with "gods."

Finally, because Barth's doctrine of woman focuses only on creation, it cannot be satisfactory. As Calvin and Luther before him, and Paul before them, Barth must understand Woman in terms of Eden and what transpired there. It is not possible to choose either creation or the Fall for a point of departure. We owe to Clause Westermann the reminder that the creation story *includes* the Fall story: creation-Fall; not creation, then Fall. The Yahwist attempts to depict the origins of his present reality, and is not really concerned with the state of human existence prior to the Fall.[36] He knows how the story is to come out. Thus it is vain to allude to the difference between the position of the woman as a helpmeet in Genesis 3:16 or equal in Chapter 1 of Genesis, and subordinate as a result of the Fall. The position of the Eve is always the same. It is her situation at the time the Yahwist is writing. Therefore, Westermann warns us, Genesis 2:18 could never be made to suggest that the man is to be the helpmeet of the woman. The order is fixed, exegetically for Westermann as it is theologically for Barth:

> The sentence does not change the fact that the woman [has always had] the fulfilment of her being, her respectability in the community, in belonging to the man, and in motherhood.[37]

To the protest of another biblical critic that "the biblical witness speaks of an ignominious servitude of the woman under her lord," Westermann responds with sensitivity only toward the text: "Ignominious . . . only if she has no children or does not belong to a man." Neither Barth nor Westermann can move beyond Paul's Genesis: Woman's only secure path to salvation is marriage, in which she is to understand herself as B, her husband as A.

✳

For Conservative and Reformation Protestantism, what is the difference between Eve's situation in Paradise, the fate imposed upon her by her sentence, her exile from Eden, and her redeemed state in Christ? The story of the Fall serves but to underline the necessity

Eve, by Antonio Rizzo; 1465–1485. Doge's
Palace, Venice. Photograph by Alinari.

of her submission to domestication: Had Eve not, for a moment, refused subordination to her husband, humanity would not have fallen; having fallen, she is sentenced to a subordination more extreme than what she had challenged; she is to work out her salvation within the boundaries of domesticity. In her family and in her church, she is to be dependent on men. The ancient dethronement of those untrustworthy and capricious female deities is ratified by the domestic order in the provisions of both Old and New Testaments. "The myth of the Fall licenses man to blame woman for all his ills, make her labor for him, exclude her from religious office, and refuse her advice on moral problems."[39]

Those who practice Judaism are obliged to live the life of faith in response to a God who is one and male. Christianity describes a life of faith that responds to a God who is one and male and incarnated in a male Christ. Roman Catholicism makes possible a holy isolation that rejects sexual expression, but Reformed Protestantism has no nuns and no developed Mariology. Thus Protestantism, like Judaism, is left with the doctrine of marriage as the framework within which Woman must be understood. Fidelity to the traditions of Genesis and the New Testament and attentiveness to the arguments of the reformers ensure that Eve will remain securely "nailed to the wall," "restrained and bridled" by her husband.

It should be understandable why some feminist scholars see gynocide (the killing of women) as a part of Christian tradition. Eve's sentence does in fact look like a form of capital punishment. The mystery plays depict Adam's frustrated, angry outburst after the expulsion from the Garden: "Would that my happy life, which flourished previously in solitude, had continued single, and had never been united to such a wife and subjected to so depraved a companion." "Mad woman, it was ill that you were ever born of me. If only the rib had been consumed in fire, which has condemned me to such confusion. When he took the rib from me, why did he not burn it and kill me?"[40] When we place our sympathies with the unhappy, put upon, "uxorious" but heroic male—as the Church Fathers, rabbis, reformers, poets, dramatists, and painters wish us to do—what is it we agree to? "Would that . . ." "If only . . ."—what? Clearly, *if only there had never been a woman at all.* For then there would have been no temptation, sin, guilt, estrangement, or punishment. And in spite of the romance with which Protestantism seeks to mitigate Eve's punishment, the remaining presumption of her guilt sustains a myth of feminine evil. "Women as a caste, then, are Eve, and are punished by a cohesive set of laws, customs and social arrangements that enforce an all-pervasive double standard."[41]

What is to be done with Eve? First of all, she must be subdued, guarded, and maintained in such a way that she can do no further harm. She must do penance for her crime by working for men who openly or secretly regard her protestations, as well as her state of subordination, with contempt. And finally, although she is obliged to participate in the drama of salvation from the sin and death she brought about (a salvation that will not free her from her sentence), she cannot be trusted with the major role in this drama. No, that part goes to a man, and that victory will be a male victory: The consequences of the sin of the First Eve can only be overcome by a Second Adam.

Adam and Eve, detail from the *Ghent Altarpiece*, by Hubert and Jan van Eyck; completed 1432. St. Bavo, Ghent, Belgium. Photograph and permission by the Institut Royal du Patrimonie Artistique, Brussells, Belgium.

8. The "Eschatological Woman"

Some righteous zeal I spent
Therefore in chiding Eve's presumption, who
When heaven and earth were all obedient
She but one woman, then just newly made
Brooked not 'neath any veil to rest content;
Beneath which veil she had devoutly stayed,
These joys past speech would have been mine to treasure
A longer time, and not so long delayed.[1]

The New Testament provides its own interpretation of the Genesis accounts of Eve's creation, sin, and punishment. The Epistles to Timothy, Titus, and the churches at Ephesus, Corinth, and Colossae comment on the character and appropriate conduct of women within the Church and society, and pointedly relate their teachings to the circumstances of the birth and fall from grace of the first woman. These *midrashim* carry for Christians the full weight and authority of Holy Scripture, and thus the importance of the view of Eve that they present, and the impact of that view on Western religion and society, can hardly be overestimated. In particular, we must pay special attention to the viewpoint of Paul the Apostle, the principal theologian of the New Testament.

Paul's theology of the body is capably and creatively presented and vigorously defended in *The Last Adam* by Robin Scroggs,[2] which features a portrayal of Jesus as a new creation that requires that the Christian give the first chapters of Genesis a new reading. Christ is said to recapitulate the first Adam but, when tempted, he remains faithful and thereby overcomes the separation, sin, and death that followed the first transgression. According to Jewish belief, which Paul certainly was familiar with and probably shared, the body of Adam was cosmic, coextensive with the created order. The second Adam, then, must similarly include all humanity within himself. As all were lost by Adam's trangression, all are now redeemed in the faithfulness unto death of the second Adam.

The significance of the death and resurrection of Jesus is thus realized in a radical notion of the unity and equality of all those who are in Christ. There can henceforth be no distinction between Jew and Greek, slave and free—and male and female. The new covenant is a revolutionary rewriting of the terms of the old, and one would expect that Paul would develop a doctrine of woman completely different from that in Genesis. In the new dispensation, it would seem that Eve is doubly blessed. First, Paul's theory of the Second Adam requires the belief that it was the First Adam who played the major role in the Genesis drama, so that it was he, not Eve, who was primarily responsible for the fall from grace. Second, if Christ has indeed overcome the sin and death of all humanity, male and female, Eve's already diminished debt in Adam has been canceled in Christ.

Now, if Paul and the young Christian community really did carry through the logic of this position, we should see in the early Church and in the New Testament evidence of a radical reassessment of the nature and status of women. In a 1972 article,[3] Scroggs examines the evidence and is immediately faced with a problem apparent to anyone reads the New Testament with care. Not only does the teaching of the early Church and the position of women within it not provide a picture of Woman freed from her Old Testament bondage, but the social and religious subjugation of women actually appears to be underscored and provided with fresh theological justification. Moreover, this theological justification is itself dependent on a particularly negative reading of Eve's role in the Genesis stories.

Scroggs confronts this problem directly and imaginatively. That the early Church insisted on the subordination of women can hardly be denied. The well-known passages from 1 Timothy (2:8-15), Titus (2:3-5), Ephesians (5:22-33), Colossians (3:18-15), and 1 Corinthians (14:33-36) all clearly demand silence and submissiveness from Christian women, and in Timothy the reason given for these restrictions is Eve's secondary status at creation and her particular guilt for the original sin. But Scroggs reminds us that these passages have been identified by biblical scholars as either certainly or very probably not from the hand of Paul.[4] He identifies as Pauline the discussion of conjugal rights in 1 Corinthians 7 and the veiling of women in 11:2-6, Galatians 3:28 concerning the equality of male and female, and scattered passages throughout the letters that greet female co-workers. Laying the foundation for his argument on textual grounds, Scroggs says that these genuine passages establish Paul as "the only certain and consistent spokesman for the liberation and equality of women in the New Testament."[5] The ideology developed by Paul, with his unifying vision of the body of Christ, represents a revolutionary doctrine of the "eschatological woman," the woman of the New Age, freed from "the subordinating rubrics of Genesis 3 and ancient society in general."[6] The Christian woman is emancipated from the social and religious burdens that attend the older, denigrating portrayal of Eve. In the Second Adam, we might say, the Christian woman becomes a Second Eve.

Scroggs maintains, however, that the early Church set aside Paul's ideas. He says that the conservative opposition could not abide so revolutionary a vision and instead enforced the terms of the old order, demanding silence and submission from women believers and leaving them to work out their salvation in married or celibate discipline. His suggestion, then, is that the Church today must return to Paul's radical gospel and reform its attitude toward women.

Temptation of Eve, by Gislebertus; ca. 1130. By permission of the Musée Rolin, Ste. Lazare, Autun, France. Photograph by G. Varlez.

Let us examine the arguments of Scroggs more closely. It is obvious, first of all, that the passages that he identifies as genuinely Pauline provide rather sparse evidence for such a unique and revolutionary doctrine of women. Is it possible that whatever the logic of Paul's Second Adam theology might require, he had no intention of altering the traditional understanding of women in Judaism and the ancient world in general? Scroggs explains that Paul might have developed the implications of his position, but "does not seem to consider the place of women a problem."[7] But even if we accept this argument, we are confronted with the evidence that when Paul does speak to the issue, his position seems more liberal than radical, more conforming than controversial, and easily placed within the spectrum of more progressive rabbinical opinion of the time. This is certainly true of his defense of equal rights and obligations within marriage, which he outlines in response to particular problems that had arisen in the Corinthian church. Then what of the famous declaration of the overcoming of the barriers between male and female? This statement would appear to be the clearest continuation of the logic of Paul's Second Adam theory. But one can also argue that it no more champions the social emancipation of women than his declaration that there is "neither slave nor free" championed the emancipation of Philemon's runaway slave, Onesimus. Paul suggested to the latter that since in Christ there is neither slave nor free, he may as well be a slave. The odd but certainly logical advice to women would seem to be that since in Christ there is neither male nor female, they may as well not aspire to the rights of males.

But we have not yet examined the linchpin of Scroggs's presentation of the eschatological woman of Paul's Christianity: his fascinating, painstaking analysis of 1 Corinthians 11:2-16. Here Paul rejects the practice among some women in the Corinthian church of praying with uncovered heads as apparently the males did. He insists that it is the position of the Church that women ought to cover their heads with veils, for "a woman ought to have *exousia* ("authority") on her head, because of the angels." Since the time of Paul, the church has understood this puzzling passage to mean that women should wear a visible sign of subordination while engaged in worship. But did Paul mean this? Scroggs argues that on the contrary, the use of the word *authority* rather than *veil* demonstrates that the purpose of the

covering is to show the liberated status of Christian women, who are
especially authorized by God to assume a position of equality with
men in worship. The wearing of the veil is a kind of credential, a
remainder to the strict constructionist opponents of Paul (whom he
nicknames *angels*) that no special restrictions should be placed on
women when they are at prayer.

This imaginative interpretation seems—alas!—forced and fanciful. Paul does, after all, introduce the subject with a reminder that
woman was created by and for man, so he surely is making the point
that she must therefore be subordinate at worship. It is true that
there is the peculiar use of *exousia* in verse 9, and that the actual
source and purpose of the veiling of women at worship is never
explained conclusively. Is Paul alluding to a pagan custom, in which
case the authority would refer to the special dignity of Roman ma-
trons, whose veils are signs of their marital status? Does Paul, perhaps, have knowledge of a long-disappeared Jewish custom whereby
women are veiled and men keep their heads uncovered at temple
observances?[8]

Tertullian's interpretation of verse 9, and the use of the word
exousia, were generally accepted by the Church; it is odd that
Scroggs does not mention it. Tertullian believed that it was derived
from a Jewish custom that connected the wearing of the veil with the
guilt of Eve.[9] We have suggested that the early Church was well
aware of the intertestamental belief that evil entered the world
through the descent of the sons of God, and further evidence for this
is the familiarity with this tradition shown by the writers of Jude (6
and 7) and 2 Peter (1:4 and 2:4). Valentinian Gnostics, who produced a "heavenly copy" of Eve in the Sophia or Zoe or Sophia-Zoe
of the *Sophia of Jesus Christ,* imagined that with the fall of Sophia a
cosmic veil was created so that "the fault of the woman should live
and she should combat error."[10]

All of this suggests that in this passage, Paul is insisting that
women should cover their heads in order to avoid a repetition of the
catastrophe that followed the incitement of the lust of the Watcher
angels at the sight of their fair heads. Scroggs, in rejecting this
explanation, is attempting to sharpen an argument of D. M.
Hooker's that is endorsed by C. K. Barrett.[11] But the original argument is neither clear nor convincing, and Scroggs does little to

Eve; detail from *Christ in Limbo,* by Sodoma; 1517. Adam and Eve lead from limbo those released by Christ in the "harrowing of hell." Pinacoteca, Siena. Photograph by Alinari.

strengthen it. Dante is closer to the truth in believing the veil to be a symbol of Eve's subjection and her refusal to wear it a sign of her rebellious nature, as is Milton, who sees it as a wedding veil. If we are to believe that Paul has developed his theology of the body into a revolutionary and truly liberating view of the eschatological woman, we will have to have better evidence than Hooker, Barrett, and Scroggs give us.

We have dealt with the argument of Scroggs at some length because it is an example of one kind of response to the feminist charge that the New Testament presents a degrading view of women. That response turns the tools of biblical scholarship to the task of finding in or providing for Scripture and tradition a more attractive attitude toward women than traditional Judaism and Christianity allow. It is ironic that an older, untutored reading of the Bible by a strong-minded feminist pioneer should have produced a conclusion that is closer to the embarrassing truth. Elizabeth Cady Stanton, her anger refined by 50 years of abuse and ridicule at the hands of Christian clergy, met at the age of 80 with a circle of women for the purpose of studying, commenting on, and correcting any passages of the Bible that provide support for notions of male superiority.[12] Without any training in textual scholarship, theology, literary or historical-critical methodology, or even biblical languages (none of the few female academics who might have helped were willing to risk their positions and reputations on so controversial a project), they nonetheless produced a provocative commentary that they boldly titled *The Women's Bible.* Their conclusions were so upsetting to suffragists—by then unwilling to risk antagonism and thus hurt the campaign for suffrage— that over Susan B. Anthony's objection the movement publicly and officially disowned the book:

> From the inauguration of the movement for women's emancipation the Bible has been used to hold her in the "divinely ordained sphere" proclaimed in the Old and New Testaments. . . . The Bible teaches that woman brought sin and death into the world, that she precipitated the Fall of the race, that she was arraigned before the judgment seat of heaven, tried, condemned and sentenced. Marriage for her was to be a condition of bondage, maternity a period of suffering and anguish, and in subjection and silence, she was to play the role of a dependent on man's bounty for all her

material wants, and for the information she might desire on the questions of the hour, she was commanded to ask her husband at home. Here is the biblical proposition of woman briefly summed up. Whatever the Bible may be made to say in Hebrew and Greek, in plain English it does not exalt and dignify women.[13]

IV. REDEMPTION

In the sixth month the angel Gabriel was sent from God to a city of Galilee named Nazareth, to a virgin betrothed to a man whose name was Joseph, of the house of David; and the virgin's name was Mary. And he came to her and said, "Hail, O favored one, the Lord is with you!" But she was greatly troubled at the saying, and considered in her mind what sort of greeting this might be. And the angel said to her, "Do not be afraid, Mary, for you have found favor with God. And behold, you will conceive in your womb and bear a son, and you shall call his name Jesus. . . ." And Mary said, "Behold, I am the handmaid of the Lord; let it be to me according to your word." And the angel departed from her.

And Mary said,

"My soul magnifies the Lord,
   and my spirit rejoices in God my Savior,
   for he has regarded the low estate of his handmaiden.
For behold, henceforth all generations
   will call me blessed."

LUKE 1:26-31, 38, 46-48

All this took place to fulfil what the Lord had spoken by the prophet:

"Behold, a virgin shall conceive and bear a son,
   and his name shall be called Emmanuel"
(which means, God with Us).

MATT. 1:22-23

And a great portent appeared in heaven, a woman clothed with the sun, with the moon under her feet, and on her head a crown of twelve stars; she was with child and she cried out in her pangs of birth, in anguish for delivery. . . . She brought forth a male child, one who is to rule all the nations with a rod of iron, but her child was caught up to God and to his throne, and the woman fled into the wilderness, where she has a place prepared by God.

REV. 12:1-2, 5-6

Then the Lord God said to the serpent . . .

"I will put enmity between you and the woman,
and between your seed and her seed;
he shall bruise your head, and you shall bruise his heel."

GEN. 3:14, 15

9. The Second Eve

Since the fresco is famous for God's right-handed reach toward Adam, no more than his right hand is noticed— as if the left were idly thrown over the back of a chair. But Michelangelo's bimane figures need watching at both extremities, and we should be missing the better half if we ignored God's alternate arm, which, without lassitude or diminution of power, embraces a winsome girl. . . . Crouched in the posture of the familiar *Venus accroupi,* she eyes God's latest invention with the keenest interest and reacts with a left-handed gesture, gripping the heavy paternal arm that weighs on her shoulder. . . .

And there is more, for being all-woman, she relates as well to the child. God's far-reaching arm, yoking her huddled form, comes to rest on a powerful putto reclined in Adamic pose, a child overscaled for his infant years and gravely serious—the only person within these biblical histories in eye contact with the beholder. Michelangelo surely meant him to represent the Second Adam, so that the span of God's arms becomes coextensive with the redemptive history of the race. And the Child's intimate nestling near to the woman's limbs makes him the son of Eve, son of the first Eve as of the Second. For the first is the type of the other: as theologians used to point out, the "Ave" by which Mary is hailed is but "Eva" reversed.[1]

Narratives in the Gospel of Luke concerning the miraculous origin of the Messiah introduce the notion that Mary, mother of Jesus, was something more than an ordinary woman. Beginning with the second century, and increasingly as the postapostolic church focused on virginity as the primary Christian virtue, Mary was considered to be a Second Eve, the exemplary redeemed woman of the new dispensation who holds out to all believers the realized possibility that sin can be overcome, death defeated, and the paradisiacal state of life with

God restored. Through the concept of the Second Eve, the First Eve acquired a character and personality that were almost—though not quite—completely new, together with a standing with God and Man she had not enjoyed even before the fateful meeting with the serpent. In the Virgin Mary are combined fully realized qualities of obedience to God and motherhood, sexual purity, and freedom from earthly vanities. Is it possible that in Mariology one may find the correction to the negative characterization of Eve at the hands of Judaism and Christianity?

⁕

In shaping the message that Jesus is the fulfillment of the messianic hopes of Judaism, the One in whom are the unique signs of God's decisive and final redemptive activity, the Church, at a very early stage, developed and preserved traditions concerning God's divine activity at the conception of Jesus. Among the prophecies of the Old Testament held to be messianic was that of Isaiah: "Behold, a virgin shall conceive and bear a son, and his name shall be called Emmanuel" (Isa. 7:14, quoted in Matt. 1:23). It is now common knowledge among biblical scholars that the Hebrew *almah,* translated into the Septuagint (the Old Testament in Greek) and then again in Matthew as *parthenos,* "virgin," is in fact more ambiguous; also that Isaiah could hardly have had in mind a prophecy of a messiah in the sense in which the early Church, possibly first century Judaism, and certainly succeeding generations of Christian theologians have viewed this passage. But early Christian apologists most certainly spoke to a belief then current that the Messiah would be virgin-born by identifying Mary, the mother of Jesus, as the Virgin.

The first teaching about Mary was not that she is the Second Eve, but that she is the Virgin Mother. It is, however, likely that the former idea was not very far from the mind of Luke; the parallels are persuasive enough in the annunciation and visitation stories.[2] Without her consort present, Mary speaks with a supernatural being (here Gabriel). She is depicted as skeptical, and we are in some suspense whether she will agree to what is proposed. She is sexually innocent. She imagines herself to be the progenitress of future generations who will recognize her singularity among women. Where

Eve is disobedient, Mary answers, "Be it done to me according to your word." In her prenatal visit to her cousin Elizabeth, she is pictured as bearing her child joyfully—in contrast to the first Eve who has been sentenced to bear children in pain. And as the First Adam gives birth to Eve not through human agency but divine intervention, Mary gives birth to the Second Adam not through human agency, but divine intervention.

Even when the evidence had to be stretched, the parallels were sufficiently suggestive to excite the imaginations of early church theologians, especially as they were given to an analysis that saw types of Old Testament figures in the characters of the New. Justin Martyr, toward the end of the first century, was the first on record with the argument that Mary should be regarded as a Second Eve:

> The firstborn of the Father is born of the Virgin, in order that the disobedience caused by the serpent might be destroyed in the same manner in which it had originated. For Eve, an undefiled virgin, conceived the word of the serpent, and brought forth disobedience and death. But the Virgin Mary, filled with faith and joy, when the angel Gabriel announced to her the glad tidings . . . answered: "Be it done to me according to thy word."[3]

It is noteworthy, remembering how the Church Fathers regarded Eve, that although the serpent is said to be the instigator of the Fall, Eve conceived his word; in other words, she is viewed as a coconspirator. It is also important to note that the crime of the first virgin is seen to be sexual in nature, and to go hand in hand with her defloration. Justin's younger contemporary, Irenaeus, was less imaginative though no less direct in drawing the parallel:

> For as Eve was seduced by the word of an angel to avoid God after she had disobeyed his word, so Mary, by the word of an angel, had the glad tidings delivered to her so that she might bear God, obeying his word. And whereas the former had disobeyed God, yet the latter was persuaded to obey God in order that the Virgin Mary might be the advocate of the virgin Eve. . . . The guile of the serpent was overcome by the simplicity of the dove, and we were set free from those chains to which we had been bound in death.
>
> As the human race was sentenced to death by means of a virgin, so it is now set aright by means of a virgin. . . . A virgin's disobedience is saved by a virgin's obedience.[4]

Detail from *The Creation of Adam,* by Michelangelo; 1511. Sistine Chapel ceiling, Vatican. Photograph by Alinari.

Once again, it is apparent that regarding Mary as a type of Eve ratifies one particular interpretation of the story of the Fall. "Seduced by the word of an angel"; "a virgin's disobedience"—this can only mean that what happened at the tree was a sexual event, namely the loss of Eve's virginity. Mary's obedience, on the other hand, involves the preservation of her virginity. Tertullian, with his legal training, therefore could see the doctrine of the second Eve as a kind of atonement that cancels out the special debt of women:

For unto Eve, as yet a virgin, had crept the devil's word, the framer of death. Equally, unto a virgin was introduced God's word, the builder of life: so that what had been lost through one sex might by the same sex be restored and saved. Eve had believed the serpent, Mary believed Gabriel. The fault which the one committed by believing, by believing the other amended.[5]

For the Fathers of the Church, Mary's virginity recalled Eve's virginal state, which was lost as both cause and effect of the fall from grace.

This interpretation of the Fall was of great importance beginning with the fourth century, when virginity became the primary ideal of discipleship. Augustine, addressing the problem of how the original sin was transmitted through the generations of humanity, saw coitus as the means by which the sins of the fathers and mothers are visited on the sons and daughters. Sin, sexuality, and death were thus woven into the tapestry depicting Eve; obedience, virginity, and eternal life became the shining attributes of Mary. And if Mary were, then *all* through virginity might be blessed. Jerome, the fourth-century champion of both virginity and the Virgin, drew the moral lesson from the Eve-Mary parallel: "Now that a virgin has conceived in the womb a child . . . the fetters of the old curse [that is, 'continually bearing children in travail'] are broken. Death came through Eve, life has come through Mary."[6] And just as the title *Christ* was added to the name *Jesus* to form one single appellation, Mary is henceforth the *Virgin Mary,* not only in testimony to God's authentic act in Jesus —the reason for which the church first spoke of Mary's virginity— but in token of her own character and as the ideal of Christian renunciation. She is transformed "from religious sign to moral doctrine."[7] Man "fallen through the woman" (Eve) may be "redeemed through the woman" (Mary), by contemplating and emulating the virginity of the latter.[8] "Everything Eve lost through her guilt Mary has won through her grace for the whole world."[9]

Identifying the Virgin Mary with Eve and seeing her as a model for holiness defined as sexual renunciation was a crucial step in the Church's understanding of Eve, as well as its characterization of Mary and its definition of the Christian life. The characterizations of Eve, Mary, and the Christian life all dealt with the questions of what Woman is, and what may be expected of her. In the first place, the sexual interpretation of the Fall became validated by the doctrine of the virginity of Mary. Paradise is virginity; the loss of virginity is the fall from grace. Mary's celibacy is her victory; Eve's disobedience is therefore her sexual defeat.

In the second place, the story of the Fall and its outcome enabled the Church—indeed, require the Church—to complete the history of Mary at those points where the New Testament falls silent or appears to contradict the perfection and beatitude of her virginity. If Eve forfeited paradise by losing her virginity, Mary as the Second Eve must secure her victory by having her virginity preserved inviolate. Her body must be "seamless, unbroken, a literal epiphany of integrity."[10] To preserve that bodily integrity became the ongoing work of Mariology. Leaving aside biblical ambiguity, contradiction, or silence, Catholic theologians relentlessly pursued the logic of the tradition of the purity of Mary. She must be seen as virginal after the conception of Jesus, preserved virginal (with intact hymen) upon his birth, and thereafter eternally virginal (aeparthenos). In 649 these dogmas were promulgated and Mary was freed forever from the penalties imposed upon Eve: desire for her husband and the painful endurance of pregnancy and childbirth.[11]

But even more was necessary. "As she had been . . . considered free of the consequences of the Fall, then it is logical to argue that she was free from the root of these consequences: original sin."[12] To achieve the full victory over sin she must, in other words, be virginal from the time of her own conception; she cannot possess, as Eve possessed, even the capacity to sin. Since she was human born, the only possibility was to declare that something miraculous and unique occurred to suspend the transmission of original sin from parent to child: an immaculate conception. Although centuries of teaching and devotion had established it unofficially as dogma, it was not until 1854 that the Roman Catholic Church made this doctrine official. And finally: To suffer the death sentence along with the primal pair for their collusion in crime would suggest that she was not the Second Eve who rejected sin. Since she was not tempted, her body should not suffer the corruption of death. She was therefore, in 1950, declared by Pius XII to have been "assumed body and soul to heavenly glory."

What remains for Mariology is for Mary to complete her apotheosis as the Second Eve by being declared equal to the Second Adam in the work of the redemption of humanity: Co-Redemptrix. But progress toward this final step was interrupted by the ecumenical interests of the Second Vatican Council, which recognized that such an action would jeopardize any possible union with other Christian groups that are scandalized by it.

Schuetzmantel-Maria aus Ravensburg, by Michael Erhart; ca. 1480. The Virgin Mary in her role as the second Eve; the protecting Mother of All Believers. By permission of the Staatliche Museen Preussischer Kultur Besitz, West Berlin. Photograph by J. P. Anders.

⁂

The doctrine of the Second Eve is supported by two biblical pillars. The first, which we have examined, depicts Mary as a type of the Eve of Genesis 3. Typologists in the postapostolic church were also drawn, inevitably, to Chapter 12 of John's Apocalypse, the Book of Revelation. There, in John's vision, "a woman clothed with the sun, with the moon under her feet, and on her head a crown of twelve stars" appears on the heavenly scene, laboring to give birth to "a male child, one who is to rule all the nations." As she cries out in her pangs, she is assaulted by a red dragon (or serpent; the Greek word is the same) who waits to devour her newborn. She flees to a desert place under the protection of God, while the child is "caught up to God to his throne." A heavenly army led by the Archangel Michael does battle against the dragon-serpent, who is cast down from heaven to earth, where he once more pursues the woman. He releases a flood of water from his mouth; the earth swallows up the river and the dragon retreats to "fight against the rest of her children, who observe the commandments of God and the testimony of Jesus."

The Apocalypse makes use throughout of the image of a woman attacked by evil personified as various beasts, with rich and complicated imagery that has tried the patience of interpreters ever since the beginning of the second century. There is no doubt that the dragon is "the ancient serpent, who is called Devil and Satan; . . . he who deceives the whole world"; this much the text tells us. Possibly the writer also has in mind the Rahab and Leviathan monster imagery of the Old Testament, probably the serpent of Genesis 3, and perhaps the more universal serpent imagery reflected in the intertestamental writings and the religious world view of the ancient Near East.[13] But who is the woman? She is depicted as heavenly and regal, but quickly becomes earthly and vulnerable. It is unlikely that the writer identified her with the Virgin Mary. Contemporary biblical scholars lean toward the view that the Apocalypse is wholly or partly Judeo-Christian in outlook ("the commandments of God and the testimony of Jesus"), and that the woman should be seen as a representative of the community of the righteous, the True Israel.[14]

The 12-starred crown marks her as a personality symbolizing the 12 tribes. Her son is less easily identified. He appears in the Apocalypse only at this place, and may or may not be the Messiah.

But before the fifth century, and particularly in centers of devotional and theological interest in Mary, the passage became attached to her and to her role as the Second Eve. Theologians recalled the role of the serpent in Genesis and in particular the curse placed on him after the Fall:

> I will plant enmity between you and the woman
> And between your offspring and hers;
> They shall strike at your head
> And you shall strike at their heel.

When an error in the Vulgate Bible transformed "they" into "she," it was understood to mean that a human woman would come in the place of Eve and strike at the head of the serpent-Satan. It seems clear, however, that the woman in the Genesis passage is Eve. The least problematic interpretation of the curse is that the Yahwist means to provide an explanation of why human beings (particularly women) seem to have an innate fear of snakes. He may perhaps also be commenting on Canaanite serpent worship. In any event, the passage certainly does not bear the eschatological significance assigned to it by the postapostolic Church.

Theological and devotional necessity, however, decided otherwise. Mariologists identified the Virgin Mary/second Eve with the woman clothed with the sun, trampling the serpent of Genesis underfoot. This provided the doctrine with the biblical sanction for her elevation to heavenly, if not divine, status. Henceforth she would be pictured crowned with the 12 stars and standing on the serpent, victorious over the tempter of her ancestral mother; the queen of the community of the faithful in the place of the progenitress of the generations of the damned. Cyril of Alexandria, opening the Council of Ephesus in 431, exulted in the victory:

Through [her] the Trinity is glorified and worshiped, the cross of the Savior exalted and honored; through [her] heaven triumphs, the angels are made glad, devils driven forth, the Tempter overcome, and the fallen creature raised up even to heaven.[15]

The significance of this mistaken identity can hardly be overestimated in its contribution to the elevation of Mary: "To admit the Virgin here is to be well on the way to finding a basis for her worship."[16] Were it not for the dynamic of the notion of the New Eve, the biblical evidence need not be marshaled to support the doctrine. The degraded Goddess, humiliated and domesticated, has been redeemed, transformed, exalted, and restored to her heavenly glory.

But Mary is the mother of Jesus, not the bride at the side of the Second Adam. Her virginity is spoken of in order to support the claim that Jesus is truly the expected Messiah; the reference to her in the creed is to support his true humanity and historicity, not hers. Yet Mariology presents her as Eve perfected in body and soul, ever the intact virgin, incorruptible on earth as in heaven, and the model for all believers. The woman clothed with the sun does not defeat the dragon, remains earthbound, and almost certainly is not the mother of Jesus. But she is now identified with Mary as the triumphant Second Eve, assumed bodily to heavenly glory. By accident and then design, however tortured, contrived, and stretched the evidence may be, the identity believed to be necessary for devotional, theological, and ethical discipleship is established. She is the Blessed Ever-Virgin, Mother of God, Queen of Heaven, and veritable image of womanhood. Whatever feminine attributes may be included in the concept of divinity are now embodied in her.[17]

⋇

What womanly attributes does the Virgin Mary represent? The identification of Mary with the Second Eve must certainly alter our picture of the prototypical woman, and therefore the ideology of women in the Western world. What does the Roman Catholic Church have in mind in its presentation of Mary as an ideal of faith and life for believers, and as a model for Christian women?

The most important characteristic of the New Eve is her virgin motherhood. It is the combination of these two apparently mutually exclusive states in one unique being that is both cause and effect of Eve's restored relationship to God; a New Eve who is held up to believers for admiration and emulation. Her virgin motherhood

The Great Red Dragon and the Woman Clothed with the Sun, by William Blake;
ca. 1805. From the Rosenwald Collection, by permission of the National
Gallery of Art, Washington, D.C.

gives religious sanction to the view that the fall of humanity was a
sexual event: The Mother of All the Living, the title Mary now
assumes, is such through virginity—without sin or lust. Eve's
disobedient loss of her virginity originated a race doomed to the loss

of its own virginity, condemned to lust. Mary's obedience originates a virginal race, freed from the curses of desire and corruption that are associated with the flesh. "Mary is . . . humanity as it would have been if there had been no Fall; Eve before her error."[18]

Not only does the activity of Mary redeem the original fallen woman, the divine activity of the Second Eve even redeems the mythology that underlies the characterization of the First Eve—the pagan notion of the Creatrix, the Mother Goddess. In Roman Catholic dogmas concerning Mary, the ancient cults of divine women are revived, refurbished, transformed, and claimed for Christianity. The pagan notion of virginity was characterized, astonishingly enough, by limitless sexual activity. "By an apparently paradoxical combination of traits, the same goddess who remains eternally virginal . . . is insatiable in her sexual appetite [and] is also the mother image."[19] The pagan goddess had scores of sexual partners whose function it was to impregnate her and thus serve the fertility cycle she represented and on which all life depended. The etymology of the word *virgin* is uncertain: It may relate to the Latin *vir* ("strength," or "life force," as in the word *virile*) in combination with *gen* (race), thus connecting it with the ancient legends of warrior-women—*viragos* or Amazons. Certainly at one time the word connoted strength and self-sufficiency, which suggested unlimited sexual activity. The idea was that having a harem of male divinities as consorts, virgin goddesses were dependent on no one male. Thus the priestesses of the goddesses who so frequently incurred the wrath of the Old Testament prophets engaged in their sexual activity in ritual emulation of their divine patronesses. To be virgin was to be thus religiously dedicated, and therefore a cult prostitute. Such —ironically—is the history of the word.

Mary's virginity, on the other hand, revolutionizes the ancient idea. In no sense can virginity involve sexual contact with men. Of the four traditional characteristics of the ancient goddesses—chastity, promiscuity, motherliness, and bloodthirstiness—Roman Catholic dogma retains only two.[20] Unlike the terrible Lilith, who is especially marked by promiscuity and blood thirstiness, Mary is utter chastity and utter motherliness. Yet she is supposed as free as the ancient goddess: As ever-virgin, she is independent of male control. She is freed from the traditional burdens of women who, as the daughters of Eve, are subject to the sentence pronounced on the primal ancestress. She can therefore turn her energies to purposes other than those of her husband. She is subject to none but God.

During the period of the Church Fathers, the meaning of virginity has still ambiguous. Adam and Eve, after all, were told to "be fruitful and multiply." Could Adam and Eve have had intercourse before the Fall and still be virgin? Some early theologians argued such a possibility, and even the Augustinian formulation does not simply equate lust with intercourse. The primal couple, in their blessed state, might have engaged in sexual activity free of lust, or in other words, virginally. But after the Fall, lust and intercourse can be disentangled only theoretically, and virginity means the absence of sexual intercourse, the proof of which in females is the intact hymen. But it was not simply—or even primarily—the conquest of sexual desire that the Church Fathers had in mind when they reflected on the meaning of Mary's virginity. The subsequent development of Mariology suggests that the Virgin became the foremost symbol of purity not because of her innocence, but because of the power of the image of the intact female body. "Wholeness," Maria Warner writes, "was equated with holiness."[21] If one recalls the story of Pandora, in which the world is polluted by Pandora's opening a jar that in some way represents her body, then the doctrine of the Second Eve can be seen as the resealing of that jar through Mary's renunciation. The corruption of sex is the corruption of death. Throughout the history of literature, artists have equated the sexually active female with disgust and sickness. When the robes are ripped from Dante's "ancient witch," a foul stench issues from her belly.[22] The bellies of Tiamat and of Spenser's dragon, Error, are loathsome and foul. And for Shakespeare's Lear, the odor of female sexuality and the darkness of the womb are demonic:

> Down from the waist they are Centaurs,
> Though women all above:
> But to the girdle do the gods inherit,
> Beneath is all the fiend's;
> There's hell, there's darkness, there's the sulphurous pit,
> Burning, scalding, stench, consumption; fie, fie, fie![23]

The Church Fathers accepted, and then refined and promoted, the common view that the female body is a mysterious vessel which, if penetrated, becomes a symbol not only of sexuality and birth but also of corruption, sin, and death.[24] Virginity preserves that body in its sealed state as a powerful symbol of Christianity's offer to humanity of the possibility of a return to a state of innocence or paradise—a sexless birth that cannot end in death. Mary's obedient chastity stands in contrast to Eve's eager acceptance of the penetration of her body, which leads to a birth which can only end in death.

But if the ancient goddess was a symbol of sexual independence the style of which Christianity could not retain, she was also a symbol of fertility: the Mother of All the Living, the giver of life. She was this even as she was a virgin. The Church Fathers were correct in believing that the ancient concept of the Mother Goddess is inherently unstable. If she is truly the *Mother Goddess* she must show motherly care for her offspring, and this must inevitably limit her sexual freedom. Thus there enters into the very nature of the goddess an element of destructiveness and terror, which her devotees recognized very well and portrayed in art and worship. To maintain her freedom, she may choose to abandon or destroy her offspring. Without some form of domestication, the sexually aggressive goddess cannot serve as a civilizing myth. She produces life, but she also constantly threatens disorder and death. Neumann provides ample evidence from ancient cultures concerning her image as a destroyer; here we need only recall the depiction of Tiamat in the *Enûma elish,* and Lilith, who must be rejected in favor of monogamous, husband-controlled, and domesticated female sexuality. Having discovered her sexuality, Eve must quickly be sentenced to bear and raise her children in subjection to Adam; only then may he give her the title of Mother of All the Living.

Roman Catholic dogma presents the Virgin Mary as an unprecedented form of the Mother Goddess. Her perpetual virginity is sexual renunciation rather than continual sexual activity; she is thus freed forever from the entanglements of sexual relationships. But she is also the Mother of All Believers. This freedom from sexual activity preserves rather than threatens her domesticity. She is the mother who will not abandon her young. The two bodily activities allowed her and celebrated in Roman Catholic piety, art, and poetry both involve caring motherhood: suckling and weeping. And because she is the true mother, she represents virtues Eve could not represent; namely obedience, gentleness, humility, and forbearance. In her independence she freely chooses domestication.

If the sexual independence of the ancient goddess called into question her ability to function as a holy mother, Mary's motherhood must call into question her sexual independence. It is fascinating to note that the notion of virgin motherhood remains as the mythical backdrop for modern moral battles of feminists. The Roman Catholic belief is that if women have control over their own bodies and are therefore free to abort potential offspring, they have reversed the triumph of the Virgin Mary over the ancient goddesses; sexual freedom is a threat to life. Mary refuses sexual freedom and is said to be truly free in her domesticity: This is the model she holds out to believers for emulation.

⎯✳⎯

What does the example of the Blessed Virgin Mother offer to Christian women? Certainly this Second Eve is characterized more positively than the First Eve. The First Eve, the self-seeking, weak-willed, disloyal temptress of Genesis is unredeemed Woman, Woman in her natural, cursed state. The Virgin Mary is Woman as she ought to be. With the concept of the Second Eve, "a great vault is thrown over the history of Western attitudes toward women; the whole mighty span resting on Eve the temptress on one side, and Mary the paragon on the other."[25]

Of course, the Virgin Mother is an ideal whose miraculous motherhood cannot really be emulated. A woman can be virgin or mother, but not both. "Mary establishes the child as the destiny of women, but escapes the sexual intercourse necessary for all other women to fulfil this destiny. Thus the very purpose of women established by the myth with one hand is slighted with the other."[26] Let us suppose, then, that emulating the virginity of the Virgin Mother, a woman chooses sexual renunciation as a profession of faith. It is true that the so-called virgin priestesses of the ancient mother goddesses were in large measure relieved of the traditional domestic burdens of women. Their holy children were communally raised, they had no husbands to serve, and they therefore could live lives of contemplation, study, religious work, and association with like-minded devotees, a choice otherwise available only to men. The price for this independence was obligatory prostitution. When that same profession was transformed into its Christian equivalent, prostitution as the price of independence became instead the renunciation of sex. This profession still provided for Christian virgins freedom from the ordinary lot of women, the liberty to develop their own lives in more creative directions. For much of human history, this freedom was usually greater than what was offered by any alternative way of life for women not born into nobility. Jerome, Anselm, and Methodius commended the virginal life for just this reason: freedom from the curse of Eve.

But they also added, significantly, that in such a virginal state women renounce womanhood, that is, they become honorary men:

> As long as a woman is for birth and children, she is different from men as body is from soul. But when she wishes to serve Christ more than the world, then *she will cease to be a woman, and she will be called man.* [27]

The state of virginity involves for women the renunciation of the ordinary female condition and, by implication, affirms a particular view of holiness that connects women with the dangers of sex. The view of holiness that requires virginity as the spiritual ideal will be discussed in the next chapter; here we must focus on its association with the doctrine of Mary's virginity. "The invincible association of holiness with physical virginity, of the power of chastity over evil, dyed the entire fabric of the Marian cult. . . . The cult of Mary is inextricably interwoven with Christian ideas about the dangers of the flesh and their special connection with women."[28] In the Christian discipline, however impressive a believer may find the character of the Virgin Mother, emulation of her involves an acceptance of a view of women that regards certain aspects of womanliness as highly undesirable.

Let us suppose that our faithful believer finds sexual renunciation, even though "better and more blessed than the bonds of matrimony," unacceptable or unrealizable. The Marian ideal then holds out its other possibility: motherhood. The Mary who is the ideal of motherhood is the Mary of the Holy Family—not at all the symbol of liberation, as the Church claims, but dutiful, submissive, and totally engaged in her domestic career. It is difficult to see in Roman Catholic descriptions of the role of the mother in the Christian family anything other than a joyful acceptance required of believing women of the curse pronounced on Eve. If the curse is instead regarded as a blessing, the duties of Christian wifehood and mother-hood will supposedly free rather than bind. In Chapter 7 we noticed that the Protestant doctrine of Woman was dependent on certain theological presuppositions about marriage, ultimately derived from the politics of Eden as described by Genesis. In a similar fashion, Roman Catholicism bases a large part of its vision of Mary on a family structure ordained in heaven: the Holy Family. The Mary who is freed from her sexuality is bound by her domesticity through this divine plan.

And it is the Natural Law of the Church, based upon Eve's sen-tence rather than Mary's victory over it, that governs female life. As Christian wife and mother, a woman is defined in terms of her subjection to her husband. Whatever hardship it may create for her, a ban on contraception ensures continued pregnancies, a ban on abortion ensures that she will bear in pain and nurture all her off-spring, a ban on divorce ensures her subjection to her husband, however intolerable the marriage may become. Her marriage may be fulfilling, but if it is not, she may only call to mind the obedience, humility, gentleness, and forbearance of the Virgin Mother.

It must surely appear to many that "the Virgin Mary is *not* the innate archetype of female nature, the dream incarnate," but rather "the instrument of a dynamic argument from the Catholic Church about the structure of society, presented as a God-given code."[29] Her "redemption" seems really to consist in her ability to bear up under her sentence:

The inimitability of the Virgin Mother model . . . has left all women essentially identified with Eve. . . . The ideal ultimately has a punitive function, since, of course, no woman can really live "up" to it. . . . Women as a caste, then, are "Eve" and are punished by a cohesive set of laws, customs and social arrangements that enforce an all-pervasive double stan-dard.[30]

10. The Countertradition:
Heretical Eves

When Eve saw Adam cast down, she pitied him, and she said "Adam, live! Rise up upon the earth!" Immediately her word became a deed. For when Adam rose up, immediately he opened his eyes. When he saw her, he said, "You will be called 'The Mother of the Living' because you are the one who gave me life."[1]

The Eve we have studied received her nature and destiny at the hands of biblical, rabbinic, and Talmudic Judaism, Roman Catholic doctrine, and Reformed Protestantism; we have called this the Western tradition. But at or on the other side of the outer limits of that tradition, voices were continually raised to challenge one aspect or another of the resultant characterization of the prototypical woman. These untraditional notions that developed alongside the more orthodox notions about Eve, often countering or tempering some of its hostility toward her, affected the characterization of Eve more than one might suspect and suggested real alternatives we are bound to consider.

We have examined the attempts of Roman Catholic Mariology and the Protestant vision of the Christian family to rescue Eve from the fate which she herself designed, or for which she was born, or to which she was misled. And we have argued that neither has succeeded in doing more than renewing the provisions of the old covenant on less stringent terms. It may be that neither Roman Catholic nor Protestant theology has thought Eve deserving or capable of anything better; certainly neither has had much doubt about her guilt. Heterodoxy, however, enlarged or altered Eve's role by raising questions about the masculine heart of the doctrine of God itself—questions that were thought by traditionalists to be fore-

closed or forbidden. In so doing, it made possible a reassessment of
her character and destiny. The most important of these reassess-
ments were provided by Shi'ite Islam (considered for our purposes
as a reformation of Judaism and Christianity), Jewish mysticism, and
Christian Gnosticism.

✳

The accounts of the Garden of Eden events in the Qur'an belong
to that lively discussion of the origin of sin that began in Jewish
intertestamental literature, and are strikingly imaginative, bold, and
learned. In the qur'anic rendition, Eve is not mentioned by name
and, as the spouse of Adam, her actions are not differentiated from
his. The first man and his wife disobey as a couple and are punished
as a couple. And, at least in the first version of the story (in *Sūra* 7),
neither seems particularly blameworthy for the human condition.

In a story interestingly paralleled by a Jewish legend, Allah com-
mands the angels to bow down to the newly created Adam (*Sūra*
7:10 ff., also alluded to in *Sūra* 17:64, 18:47, and 20:115). Iblis
(Satan) refuses and for that reason is banished from heaven. He
vows to "sit in ambush" and await the moment to avenge himself
on the couple. The opportunity presents itself when the man and
woman are commanded by Allah not to eat of the fruit of one of the
trees, without being told why. Satan whispered to them, to reveal
to them what was hidden from them of their shameful parts," claiming to be "a sincere adviser" (7:19). They understand this to mean
that they should disobey Allah and eat the fruit, and when they do
so "their shameful parts [are] revealed to them" (7:21). As punishment for taking the advice of Satan, Allah pronounces the man and
woman enemies "each to each" and sends them to earth, where they
are to "live and die and from [where] they will be brought forth"
(7:24).

The parallel account in *Sūra* 20:115 f. suggests a greater degree
of responsibility on the part of the couple, for they are warned prior
to the temptation not to listen to Satan. After they succumb and are
cast down to earth, they are offered forgiveness if they will but
follow the guidance of Allah. As his "children," that is, those who
hear the Qur'an, they are admonished not to "be like the Satans"

and commit "indecency," as "He brought your parents out of the
Garden, stripping them of their garments to show them their shameful parts."

The accounts clearly relate eating from the mysterious tree with
the knowledge of why it is that the genitals are shameful, and therefore with sexuality. To the drama of the biblical account, the Qur'an
adds the removal of clothes from a couple whose original, proper
state is clothed. But no special role is assigned to the woman. It is
Arabic poetry and *hadith* ("tradition") literature that places Eve,
now by name, under the familiar shadow. With the important exception that the traditional analysis contains no explicitly sexual *haggada*,
Islamic treatment is not unlike Judaic; and, as the examples in
Schwarz's study show, the characterization of Eve is not notably
different from that in Christian history. "The first man who suffered
loss and underwent pain and trouble for obeying a woman was
Adam, who did the bidding of Eve," writes Nizan al-Mulk (d.
1096).[2] Woman is incorrigible, since "she is made of a crooked rib,"
holds an early tradition.[3]

There is thus little justification for the claim of Muslim apologists
that the qur'anic version of the Fall story, because it does not specifically accuse Eve, makes possible for Islam a more positive assessment
of women; whatever a thoughtful Muslim may practice, both the
Qur'an and the *hadith* consistently emphasize the superiority of men
over women "on account of the qualities with which Allah has gifted
the one above the other" (*Sura* 4:38). Women suspected of harbor-
ing rebellious thoughts are, according to the well-known passage in
the Qur'an, to be banished to their rooms and beaten. The function
of women is to serve men and to propagate the species; in the famous
figure of speech, they are "fields for plowing," "tillage" (2:223),
and in no sense the guardians of their own sexuality or earthly affairs.
It is true that the Qur'an is unusually preoccupied with the regula-
tion of domestic affairs and thus with the rights of women, but it is
only in comparison to pre-Islamic conditions that the *sharia* (religious laws) can be regarded as enlightened. The noted Islamicist
Ignaz Goldziher remarks that "Islam itself placed women, as even
its eager apologists must admit, far lower than men on the social
scale; women are called 'the majority of those in Hell, '. . . i.e.,
lacking in religion and understanding.'"[4] And Islam remains in its

An Islamic Adam and Eve, by Manafi al-Hayawan; 1294–1299. Maragha,
Iran. By permission of the Pierpont Morgan Library, New York.

visible expressions characteristically—indeed, extraordinarily—patriarchal.

Still, there are features of Islamic tradition that develop the motif of Eve in directions that can only strike a Westerner as astonishing. So stringent is the requirement that Allah be wholly other than man that Islam cannot admit a conception of God as father. But the harshness of this doctrine of God (to the Jew or Christian) is tempered somewhat by the application of honorific titles until, according to tradition, 99 are accumulated. What is noteworthy is that the great majority of these names are female or reflect female characteristics. Feminine aspects of love that cannot be allowed between Allah and his people may be suggested within the life of Allah himself.

It is also significant that Miriam (Mary), the mother of Jesus, is regarded by the Qur'an and therefore by all Muslims as one of those figures from biblical tradition (like Adam and Eve, Abraham, Moses, and Jesus) who assume a kind of coloration of divinity. To consider even Muhammad divine would be *shirk,* the worst of heresies, for there is none like or beside Allah. Nevertheless, the veneration of Mary is an important aspect of Islam.[5] In the Qur'an, she is the only woman referred to by name. She is presented as a paradigm of virtue, purity, and submission, "chosen and purified by Allah" (*Sura* 66:12), and particularly praiseworthy for "guarding her virginity" (*Sura* 21:90, 66:13). The striking accounts of the conception and birth of Jesus—who, it must be remembered, is regarded as a *rasul* or divine messenger like Adam and Eve and Muhammad himself— parallel in many respects the story in Luke. In addition to this, there are echoes in the birth story of the woman of Revelations who is clothed with the sun: the withdrawal to a distant place for the birth, the terrible labor pangs, and the motif of the river (Rev. 19:20-24, 3:31f.).

But the development of a concept resembling that of the Second Eve of Christianity begins not with Miriam, but with legends surrounding Fatima, historically the youngest daughter of Muhammad and the wife of his cousin Ali. Fatima gradually became "the embodiment of all that is divine in womanhood and the noblest ideal of human conception."[6] It is noteworthy that even the *Sunni,* the traditionalists, do not reject the *hadith* in which Fatima is declared to be "queen of the women of Paradise next to Miriam." In fact, she collects around her personality aspects of traditions that Judaism and Christianity associate with Eve or the Virgin Mary. Her favored title is *al-Zahra,* "the Shining One," and in popular piety she and Ali function as a kind of primal couple. They are also the ultimate couple; in the eschatology of certain sects of Islam, they are leading characters in the drama of the final days.[7]

In the turmoil over the succession to Muhammad, one party championed the blood inheritance through Ali and Fatima. The failure of this group, which subsequently became the second major group of Islam alongside the *Sunni,* the *Shi'a,* rent Islam asunder and the martyrdom of Fatima's two sons at the hands of the *Sunni* marked the schism with blood. The martyr-conscious *Shi'a* thus place Fatima at the center of an eschatological vision, imagining her reappearance as heralding the arrival of the final successor, the last imam or *Mahdi,* who will renew the faith and rule personally by divine and blood right. Accordingly, much of the development of the Fatima legend has been at the hands of the *Shi'a.*

We learn that Muhammad is told by a heavenly being before Fatima's conception that she will be pure and blessed, and that the imams who succeed him will be born from her. He is said to receive from an angel, or to pick from a tree inhabited by her spirit, an apple or a date that he eats, which is transformed in his loins into a spermatic fluid with which he then impregnates his wife. When Fatima is born, she is attended by celestial beings, including Miriam. The gifts of property included in her bride price are paradise and hell, over which she therefore exercises control. She is exempt from the physiological troubles of women such as menstruation, labor, and menopause, and gives birth to her sons through her thigh, thus preserving her virginity—for which she is called *al-Batul,* "the Virgin." She is also called *al-Muhaddatha* because she is told by the angels that "Allah has chosen and purified you; he has chosen you from among the women of the world." Perhaps the most intriguing of her titles is *Umm Abiha,* "mother of her father," so-called because the last imam will be called Muhammad, like her father and her younger son.

It would be incorrect to see in all this an Islamic Mariology, but clearly there has been a more active interchange of ideas between Islam, Judaism, and Christianity than any of them has cared to admit.

It is also certain that the Islamic idea of the 99 names and the legends surrounding Fatima temper the proscription against the Divine Feminine all three faiths insist on. From popular piety and folklore we therefore have ideas within Islam that reassess positively the character of Eve. In the stories concerning Fatima, we can also see the foundation for that characteristic courtly romanticism of Islamic literature; the high valuation of the company of women:

> Woman, synthesizing in her substance virgin nature, the sanctuary and spiritual company, is for man what is most loveable; in her highest aspect, she is the formal projection of merciful and infinite inwardness in the outward, and in this regard she assumes a quasi-sacramental and liberating function.[8]

But history has taught us that this kind of idealization of women usually conceals both control and contempt. To serve a liberating function is not the same thing as being liberated. The symbol of this confusion is, of course, the veil. Is the veiling of women, which is particularly important for Shi'ism, a token of Islam's high regard for women, or of masculine control of their destinies? It is, of course, both. In the influential theory of civilization developed by al-Ghazali (1050-1111), as Fatima Mernissi writes,[9] work and civilization depend on satisfied sexuality. But satisfied sexuality is controlled sexuality; whereas the Western world regards men as active and women passive, in Islam the opposite is true. "Sexual desire was created solely as a means to entice men to deliver the seed and to put the woman in a situation where she can cultivate it, bringing the two together softly in order to obtain progeny, as the hunter obtains his game."[10] What is feared is that female sexuality will demand more than this. Ghazali "sees civilization as struggling to contain the woman's destructive, all-absorbing power. Women must be controlled to prevent men from being distracted from their religious and social duties. Society can survive only by creating the institutions which foster male dominance through sexual segregation."[11]

Women are thought to possess *qaid,* "the power to deceive and defeat men, not by force, but by cunning and intrigue."[12] Because they have *qaid,* women can bring about *fitna,* which is highly feared. *Fitna* is the word for disorder, chaos, and the uncontrollable sexuality believed to be embodied in women. To desegregate Islamic life would release that sexuality and destroy Allah's order.[13]

Illustration from *Chronology of Ancient Peoples,* by al-Biruni; 1307–1308, Iran. The story is confused with Zoroastrian features. In place of the serpent, Ahrıman offers a magical fruit that restores youth. Islamic injunctions against idolatry made artistic representations of its prophets very rare, and the depiction of two of them unclothed was possible only during the liberal Persian period. The artist has adopted the Christian convention. By permission of the University of Edinburgh Library.

In the final analysis Islam's Eve, though she has shadings of divinity, is not an attractive religious figure.

⁓⋇⁓

Ancient Judaism also discovered that the motif of the Feminine could not really be exterminated as a religious idea, whatever the requirements of a stringent monotheism. The divine female remained to threaten the Oneness of Yahweh and his created order. In the liturgy Yahweh again and again had to do battle against those powers—personified and reified as female—that threatened both his majesty and his creation. The prophets pronounced time and again against the apparently inevitable recurrences of the worship of the banished gods of neighboring religions—Asherah, Astarte, and Anath or the Queen of Heaven.[14] Judaism (like Islam) could not finally allow a truly independent female deity alongside the male divinity, however, and it is not within consensus Judaism that we should seek a reassertion of the power of the Feminine. This had to come in more heterodox expressions of the faith, and even there from within the doctrine of the male God.

If it was not permissible for Judaism to employ sexual imagery to describe the relationship between God and his creation, it was nonetheless possible that manifestations of him and emanations from him could exhibit and develop female characteristics. We noted a similar development in Islam with the 99 names. Wisdom, the Torah, and the Holy Spirit (for example) came to be characterized by Jews as female, partly, but not solely, because the words for them were feminine in gender. As religious concepts came to be personified for narrative purposes, it became possible for aspects of God

Eve and the Serpent, by William Blake; undated. By permission of the Victoria and Albert Gallery, London.

—some of them thought of as female—to assume independent roles within the Godhead.

The most interesting and most famous development along these lines resulted in the *Shekhina,* or "indwelling" of God in his creation.[15] The notion of the *Shekhina* combines mystical, devotional, doctrinal, and romantic ideas. The basic assumption is that the community of Israel in its suffering exile retains, as the realization of Yahweh's promise to be with his people, a divine presence that experiences what the people themselves experience, even though in his incomprehensibility and inapprehensibility God's independence from them is secure. In effect, a part of God is exiled from himself; a daughter wanders in far lands, seeking reunion with him.[16] Thus, "to lead the *Shekhina* back to her Master, to unite her with him, is in one way or other the true purpose of the *Torah.*"[17] That reunion or redemption is regarded by mystical Judaism as a return to the original wholeness of creation.

The *Zohar,* the masterpiece of *Kabbalah,* is never certain whether sin was the actualization of a potential evil by the actions of Adam and Eve, or part of the original act of creation itself, which involved a series of separations. Thus evil, in *Kabbalah,* appears to have a mysterious, magical existence of its own, given life when Adam throws the various elements of creation out of their natural balance.[18] Adam's sin is said to have "interrupted the stream of life which flows from sphere to sphere and brought separation and death into the world. From this time on there has been a mysterious fissure, not indeed in the substance of divinity but in its life and action."[19] The end will thus be only the beginning once again; "Only after the restoration of the original harmony in the act of redemption, when everything shall once again occupy the place it originally had in the divine scheme of things, will 'God be one and his name one,' in biblical terms, truly and for all time."[20]

One might think of the long development of *Kabbalah* as a meditation on the legend of the separation of the primal waters of creation, whereby the upper and lower waters were personified as lovers interrupted by God and forbidden to resume their intercourse. God's purpose is to create a space for civilization, for the life of humanity; his providential care is the maintenance of the separation lest the primal waters come back together. God's providence secures his creation against chaos, although it is a central characteristic of Kabbalist thinking that a special divine pulse is sensed in just that chaos. The end of time is the relapse, the end-beginning, both feared and longed for. History, as we said in the first chapter, is a *coitus interruptus.*

It is important to understand redemption in such sexual terms if we are to understand the explicitly erotic language of the *Zohar* in the face of the traditional compunctions of Jewish theology. The *Shekhina* becomes in the *Zohar* "a palpable individuum whose acts, words and feelings only make sense if she is considered a true mythological deity."[21] Within the Godhead, she is wedded to her husband-twin, the king, and the life and welfare of humanity is mirrored in a divine marital relationship. When the temple, "the bridal chamber," is destroyed, the king "withdrew into the remote height of heaven and made himself inaccessible."[22] The *Shekhina,* however, remains on earth with her people as the embodiment of the community of Israel. Here she suffers the vicissitudes of earthly existence. Because Israel is prone to sin, Samael, the Evil One who always lies in wait seeking his opportunity, is empowered to enjoy her. The king, for his part, must take a substitute partner who is identified as none other than Lilith—here a symbol for Christianity. Thus God suffers with his people by being deprived of honor, respect, and his rightful relationship with them.

These mysteries have for *Kabbalah* a devotional rather than an intellectual significance (if such a distinction can be made for *Kabbalah*), since "everything that is done by the individual or the community in the mundane sphere is magically reflected in the upper region, i.e. a higher reality which shines through the acts of man." At the center of this ethical system is *devekuth,* an "adhesion" or union with God which, unlike the usual ecstatic experience of mysticism in other religions, is realized in normal individual and social life.[23] Close to its center is the sexual life of marriage. On the night of *Shabbat* pious couples cohabit "in full cognizance of performing a most significant act in direct imitation of the union which takes place at that very time between the Supernal Couple. . . . By doing so they set in motion all the generative forces of the mythico-mystical universe."[24] This, Scholem reminds us, reflects the positive attitude Judaism has always shown toward the function of sexual life and its consistent rejection of asceticism and celibacy. "Every true marriage is a symbolical realization of the union between God and the *Shekhina*."[25]

The relevance of these developments in mystical Judaism to the history of the Eve tradition should be clear. Here we have what appears to be a consideration of religion that focuses on life not as a banishment from paradise, but as a metaphor for the restored paradisiacal unity; the creation is more important than the Fall. Particularly attractive is the positive valuation of human sexuality as an expression of that unity. But a closer look raises the question of whether Jewish mysticism is truly a reassessment of the tradition, particularly as regards the role of women. Adam's sin is said to be that he failed to discern and preserve the original unity of the *Sefiroth,* the divine attributes or aspects that comprise the Godhead. Instead, he "separated one from the other and set his mind to worship the *Shekhina* only without recognizing its union with the other *Sefiroth.*"[26] Hidden in this statement, ignored by Scholem, is the belief that the original copulation in paradise was not an activity that participated in the whole of the deity, and thus in the whole of creation. Human sexuality includes, at its heart, the awareness of separation and alienation, and the unification that takes place in the sex act is disturbing to the extent to which it is a reminder of disunity. This is a profound insight in *Kabbalah,* but let us see how it is developed.

We notice the familiar characters of the Adam and Eve legends: Samael, lying in wait for Eve, and Lilith, united here, basely but inexorably, with the king. With the magical realm of the demonic substituted in *Kabbalah* for a clear conception of sin and evil, it is worth nothing the proximity of that realm to the aspect of the *Shekhina:*

> It is of the essence of Kabbalistic symbolism that woman represents not, as one might be tempted to expect, the quality of tenderness but that of stern judgment. . . . The demonic, according to the Kabbalists, is an offspring of the feminine sphere.[27]

The feminine element in God turns out to be far more complex than his masculine aspect; "innumerable strands of attraction and repulsion run back and forth."[28] The feminine portion of the Godhead is Eve and Lilith, God and Devil. The religious and sexual experience of *Kabbalah* is thus highly ambivalent, precisely because it tries to be a sexual vision that encompasses the religious. The psychological insight it possesses is akin to the visions of Freud and Roheim, where everything is seen solely from the point of view of the striving male, and destruction is bound closely to the sought reunion.

Both historically and metaphysically it is a masculine doctrine, made for men and by men. . . . This exclusive masculinity for which Kabbalism has paid a high price, appears rather to be connected with an inherent tendency to lay stress on the demonic nature of woman and the feminine element of the cosmos.[29]

In the past 40 years, many new writings of Gnostic Christianity have been discovered, translated, and analyzed. The orthodox apologists of the first centuries of the Church had called Gnostic Christianity that "abyss of madness and of blasphemy," and its adherents were characterized as "agents of Satan," "schismatics," "heretics," "spreading . . . the bitter and malignant poison of the great Serpent, the great author of apostasy."[30] Now that we have available to us many of the actual writings of that movement, which produced the first great Christian heresies, we cannot simply accept the versions of Gnostic teachings provided by the apologists. It is clear that we can no longer speak with confidence of the "Church" of the first four centuries and the "Gnosticism" that it opposed; much of what the apologists condemned as unacceptable was regarded by even their more traditionalist contemporaries as authentically Christian teaching. The situation of early Christianity was simply much more fluid—indeed, confused—than has been acknowledged, and much of what later became Christological, ecclesiological, and moral doctrine is indebted to Gnostic teachings.

Gnosticism—the name itself a label given by its enemies to a wide variety of viewpoints that seem at first to have little in common but complicated, often impenetrable mythologies—assumed that knowledge of God and the self was intuitive, but that only the properly prepared and enlightened could receive and understand the saving mysteries.[31] Depending on the particular school of thought, it was believed that preparation and enlightenment might come through asceticism or libertinism, the eating of certain foods or the avoidance of certain foods, celibacy or sacred marriage, or participation in elaborate rituals. What the various adherents had in common was a spontaneity of expression, and indifference or contempt toward the notion of the authority of Scripture or apostolic tradition or church hierarchy. Some Gnostic schools openly rejected Christianity, others claimed to be the true Christianity, and still others maintained the outward forms and practices of orthodoxy but met secretly with their own books and ritual practices. It was the two latter types of groups that forced the issue of what ought to be considered genuinely Christian and what ought to be rejected as contrary to the saving message.

Most Gnostics were fascinated with the question of how an evil universe could be related to a perfect divinity, and how one could dwell in the former and attain to the latter. They were therefore bound to be keen students of the first chapters of Genesis, producing theories about the origin of God and the universe at the very point where the Old Testament refuses speculation for fear of compromising monotheism. Finding too many questions left unanswered, and having no such fear, the Gnostics declared that the apparent world had already compromised belief in Yahweh. Many Gnostics believed that such a world could only be the result of generations of emanations from the Primal Source, each progressively less perfect; one of which eventually erred and produced the agent of creation, the flawed God of Judaism. The world thus was created evil by a divinity who fell away from, or was never a part of, the *Pleroma,* the divine fullness that alone has true existence.

Gnosticism imagined a cosmic catastrophe as the mythological metaphor for the human predicament. It is here that Eve—most often given other names, but still recognizably the character of the biblical story—has her history rewritten. Her plight is once more a heavenly rather than an earthly one, but a plight bearing the profoundest significance for life on earth. Female embodiments of the Godhead abound in the Nag Hammadi treasury of Gnostic writings —Barbelo, Hyle, Nous, Sophia, Norea, Prunicos, Achamoth, Sophia-Zoe, Eve, Zoe-Eve, and Eden.[32] We would have to go far beyond the limits of this study to organize and investigate in any detail the complicated and rich mythopoetic material in the Gnostic ideas of the cosmologically and religiously feminine. It must suffice to say that, in general, these tendencies typically introduced such ideas at that point when the world, or the creator of the world, was generated; that is, the concept of the feminine bridged the chasm between the perfection of divinity and the corrupt world. Thus Sophia (Wisdom) falls when she attempts to imitate the creative power of the Supreme Principle, or when she attempts to comprehend the mystery of the originating power, thereby producing a defective thought or offspring.

The most highly developed mythology concerning the descent and ascent of Sophia occurs in the writings of the Valentinian school, probably the most influential and certainly the most theologically interesting of the Gnostic Christian groups. Alternate theories viewed the concept of the Feminine similarly in their attempts to account for the cosmic origin of evil. *Baruch,* by the Gnostic teacher Justin, posits three "unbegotten principles" in the universe; two male ("Good" and "Father") and the third female ("Eden" or "Matter": "without foreknowledge, wrathful, double-minded, a virgin above and a viper below.").[33] In *Exegesis on the Soul,* Nous (Spirit) is female, though she is also described as androgynous; she falls "down into a body" and is defiled and seduced by many and given sickly offspring.[34] In the Sethian-Ophite system, Sophia generates Ialdabaoth, the cosmic serpent who struggles with her as she assists and advises Adam and Eve.[35] In the *Second Treatise of Seth* she is described as Ialdabaoth's enemy and a whore,[36] and it is Ialdabaoth who seduces the heavenly Eve in the *Apocryphon of John,* impregnating her with the defective deities Elohim and Yahweh and "planting sexual desire in her who belongs to Adam [that is, the earthly Eve]."[37]

The mythology of the Gnostics is clearly indebted to the biblical story of the Fall and the interpretations of the role of Eve in intertestamental writings and contemporary rabbinical schools. G. C. Stead argued in 1969 that the Valentinians, in particular, were heavily dependent on Philo, attenuated versions of the popular Isis cult, Pythagorean speculations, neo-Platonism, and early Christian trinitarian formulations, and less on the Genesis traditions.[38] But

Where Do We Come From? Who Are We! Where Are We Going? by Paul Gauguin; 1897. The artist has incorporated many features from representations of Eve painted throughout his career, and places her here in a society of women. See Wayne Anderson, *Gauguin's Paradise Lost* (New York: Viking, 1971) and Henri Dorra, "The First Eves in Gauguin's Eden," *Gazette des Beaux-Arts* 41 vol. (Paris, 1953): 182–202. By permission of the Boston Museum of Fine Arts.

George W. MacRae has said the Gnostics owed far more to the story of the Fall and to the Watcher and Wisdom traditions of Judaism, and the rapid growth of knowledge about Gnosticism during the past ten years has tended to support his contention.[39] Jewish tradition had already associated Wisdom with the act of Creation, and intertestamental writings, with their tendency to hypostasize divine concepts, assigned Wisdom and Spirit the female gender. We have previously examined intertestamental writings about a fall of divine beings bringing about evil. MacRae concludes that "the very intention of the Gnostic myth [of Sophia] is to provide a 'true,' esoteric explanation of the Genesis story itself."

Jewish tradition from biblical times onward had a keen sense of the disorder in the world resulting from the fall of the first couple from the state in which they had originally been constituted. Now the Gnostic, who began with the more radical notion that the world itself was disorder, would seek to explain this situation by postulating a fall in the Pleroma of which the fall of man is but an inferior copy. But the correspondence is not quite as straightforward as this statement implies, for often the Gnostic "midrash" perverts the whole intention of the biblical story, as it does in this instance in the *Apocryphon of John* and other works, by showing that the fall of man from paradise was actually beneficial for man, at least in its intent, since it was an attempt to liberate him from the power of the Archons. Man could only begin to rise to the supreme God when he had left the clutches of the Jewish creator-God.[40]

Sophia is the cause of the fall of humanity, just as the Eve of Genesis is the cause; they both try to be like God.

But if the redivinized Eve of Gnosticism enters its mythologies at the point where the corrupt world or its corrupt Creator comes into being, we also have in those same and many other Gnostic writings another apprehension of the Feminine as a religious concept, one that has attracted much interest from feminist theologians. The supreme, originating power may appear in dyadic form, that is, as a male or sexless being together with a consort. In the *Apocryphon of John* there is Barbelo, the "shine" (compare the Hebrew description of the *Shekhina*) of the ineffable light of the primal force, "the perfect power which is the image of the invisible, virginal spirit"; "the womb of everything for she is prior to them all, the Mother-Father."[41] The androgynous Adam is created by Sophia-Zoe in *On The Origin of the World,* patterned after his mother, "Eve of Life," who is the "Instructor of Life," the "Mother of Living."[42] Sophia-Zoe is thus at one stroke the virgin wife, mother, and daughter of her husband-son-father, Adam, and the midwife and physician of humanity. In the *Hypostasis of the Archons,* the woman who is taken from the side of Adam comes to him, and he rises at her command and pronounces her "Mother of the Living," "Physician," "Woman," "She-Who-Has-Given-Me-Birth." A female spiritual principle appears in the form of the snake-instructor and advises the couple to eat the fruit, thus thwarting Samael/Ialdabaoth, the ignorant and arrogant power of this world.[43] There are many similarities between Eve's song in *On the Origin of the World* and the long, extraordinary poem put in the mouth of an unnamed female in *The Thunder, Perfect Mind:*

> For I am . . . the honored one and the scorned one
> I am the whore and the holy one
> I am the wife and the virgin
> I am the mother and the daughter
> I am the members of my mother. . . .
> I am the bride and the bridegroom and it is my

husband who begot me
I am the mother of my father and the sister of my
husband and he is my offspring.[44]

It must certainly appear as though the Gnostics were attempting to redress that cosmic sin committed by the writers of Genesis and compounded by the doctrines of the early Church: the banishment of the Feminine as a divine category. Religious theorists seeking to defend the Jungian notion of the archetype will find here much that is attractive, supporting the belief that preconscious humanity dealt with the sacred as a union of opposites; thus the Great Mother is seen as virgin and whore, daughter and mother, creator and destroyer, bringer of life and death. Stead and MacRae prefer a more modest explanation of the appearance of opposing values in single person-ages and conceptions in the Gnostic writings. Already in Philonic conceptions of the *Logos* and *Sophia,* there is considerable ambiguity because Wisdom and the Word were generating principles and therefore sacred at the same time that they were bridges to an imperfect world and therefore in touch with the corrupt. Only an extemely ambivalent cosmic personality could have served the Gnos-tics as the agent of creation, so vast was the gulf to be bridged. Most often, the opposing tendencies simply could not be reconciled into one personality, resulting in upper and lower Sophias, or the intro-duction of other satellite personalities that incorporated some attri-bute. One could say of practically any Gnostic theologian what Stead has written about Valentinus: "Faced with a range of divergent conceptions, he was unable either to select or combine them."[45] Often in Gnostic writings, then, what may appear to be a profound affirmation of a coinciding of opposites might be better recognized as unresolved theological and literary ambiguity.

One theme that recurs in several of the writings is a view of Eve's role as adviser or counselor. Here we should recall two interpreta-tions of Eve's name, *hawwāh:* "Mother of All the Living" and "Ser-pent-Mother." Several Gnostic writings favor a third possibility: *hawwāh,* the *ezer* of Adam, is his "adviser" (from the Aramaic *hawa,* "to instruct"). The Talmud and intertestamental writings had also made this connection, but neither suggested that the wordplay sup-ported anything other than a negative view of her character. The advice that she gives is, after all, bad advice, and the wordplay completes the circle of her conspiracy with Satan: ḥawwāh (Eve) = ḥawa (adviser) = ḥewya (serpent). In some Gnostic stories it is the serpent itself who advises, and it is to this tradition that the Qur'an appears to be indebted: In *Sura* 7, the Satan-snake offers himself as a "sincere adviser."[46]

Were some Gnostic groups attempting a positive reassessment of Eve's role as adviser? We have strong evidence that one feature of Gnosticism that distinguished it from more traditional Christian groups was a policy of egalitarianism toward its adherents. Women occupied positions of theological and ecclesiastical leadership, and Elaine Pagels, in *The Gnostic Gospels,* maintains that the Gnostics were persecuted and finally harried out of the Church partly because male-dominated Christianity was unwilling to allow women in positions of authority.[47] The Gnostic attitude toward women in their own communities and what appears to be a Gnostic tendency to restore the Feminine to the divine realm in its theology have been of considerable interest to contemporary feminist theologians.

The extent to which women were prominent in community leadership and in developing the actual theology of Gnosticism remains to be determined. We can, however, address the question of why the role of the female characters in the Gnostic dramas of salvation is so ambivalent. For every affirmation of the Feminine in Gnostic mythology, there is a "nevertheless." The *Valentinian Exposition,* for example, asserts that the "correction" of Sophia "will not occur through anyone except her own Son [i.e., Jesus] who alone is the fullness of divinity."[48] The *Exegesis of the Soul* promises a messianic bridegroom-brother who will come to restore the unfortunately incarnated Nous, though how this is to take place is not explained.[49] In the *Gospel of Thomas,* Peter's remark concerning Mary that "women are not worthy of life" is met by Jesus' promise to lead Mary "in order to make her male, so that she may become a living spirit resembling you males, for every woman who will make herself make will enter the Kingdom of Heaven."[50]

It is, in fact, the latter notion that is prevalent in the Gnostic writings, which sets a large question mark after contemporary feminist approval of Christian Gnosticism. "Flee from the madness and the bondage of femininity, and choose for yourselves the salvation of masculinity."[51] The Savior has come "to destroy the works of femaleness."[52] The primary work to be destroyed seems to be the very existence of women as women. How is this contradiction, which cuts through the heart of Gnostic writings, to be explained?

For Gnosticism, the existence of Woman is the ever-present reminder of the primal separation. Before she was separated out from Adam and the "glory" departed, Mankind was asexual, bisexual, or angelic.[53] The separation is regarded as the destruction of a perfect world for which the woman is held to be at fault. But Gnosticism also offers a way by which the separation can be overcome and the unity of paradise restored: Eve can be assimilated back into Adam.

To understand what Gnosticism means by regarding Eve as an adviser and female believers as of equal stature with male believers, we must examine the notion of *syzygia*. Some schools of Gnosticism believed that the angelic unity could be recovered through the discipline of spiritual, sexless pairings of male and female believers. Certainly chapters 68 through 70 of the *Gospel of Philip* must be read as descriptive of these celibate marriages:

> When Eve was still in Adam death did not exist. When she was separated from him death came into being. If he again becomes complete and attains his former self, death will be no more. . . .
>
> If the woman had not separated from the man, she would not die with the man. His separation became the beginning of death. Because of this Christ came to repair the separation which was from the beginning and again unite the two. . . . But the woman is united to her husband in the bridal chamber. Indeed, those who have united in the bridal chamber will no longer be separated. Thus Eve separated from Adam because she was never united with him in the bridal chamber.[54]

This Valentinian tract provides the mythologized basis for the practice of virginal marriages between believers ("undefiled marriage . . . not fleshly, put pure").[55] The Fall is seen to result from, or to result in, sexuality, a "fall into the body." Gnostic Christianity therefore seeks a return to paradise, by which is meant the original androgynous or sexless state of the angels, through the discipline and ritual of the *sponsa Christi*, the bride of Christ or the spiritual *syzygia*. The original humans were meant to live together as angels, who are both sexless and immortal. But the creation of Eve or the first intercourse involved them in bodily life, resulting in corruption and death. Thus, the characteristic equation of Gnosticism.:

While normal sexuality in fact allays or forestalls the effects of death upon the race by bringing new life to birth, in the elemental metaphysic of Gnosticism the terrible cyclic argument of the human condition, that of "birth, copulation and death," was only to be broken by the removal of the middle term.[56]

Much of this teaching about sexuality and the necessity of over-coming the work of women Christian monasticism held in common with Christian Gnosticism. Woman was "the work of Satan" for Epiphanius, for whom virginity was the "cornerstone of the church."[57] Gnostic Christianity and Christian monasticism shared the conviction of *The Apocryphal Gospel of the Egyptians,* which asked, "How long shall men die?" and answered, "So long as women bear children."[58] Therefore, women should choose the virginal profes-sion so that their work might be overcome and (this time in the words of Jerome) they might "become men." To the monastic mind, the ideal of celibacy, the higher state, was to be reached in solitude or in a sexually segregated community. Gnostic Christianity added a third possibility: the community of sexless marriage of the New Adams and the New Eves.

The heart of *syzygia* was probably a discipline not unlike the ancient Hindu *brahmacharya,* which Gandhi practiced, particularly in his later years, much to the consternation of his senior lieutenants. Sexual asceticism could only be regarded as a saintly virtue by con-tinually being put to the test, and Gandhi took to sleeping with young women in his entourage to prove his own commitment to celibacy. His followers were horrified at the prospects for scandal that could be seized upon by the opposition. The Christian apolo-gists, whose celibate communities were strictly segregated by sex, probably could not believe that the *syzygia* of this form of Gnosticism were anything other than further proof of the licentiousness com-mon in other Gnostic groups, who believed that the recovery of paradise could be realized by free, nonreproductive sexual activity of the kind supposedly engaged in by Adam and Eve before the Fall. They certainly succeeded in presenting all of Gnosticism as sexually dissolute, and with their victory, the desert solitude of St. Anthony won out over the *syzygia* of Jesus as New Adam and Mary as New Eve as the model for the monastic life.

Eve as helpmeet, as adviser, as half of the dyadic diety or of the earthly *syzygia,* found an undoubtedly important place in the Gnostic scheme. This made possible an egalitarian attitude toward women in the life, worship, and governance of the communities, as well as the restoration of the Feminine, in many guises and forms, in the mythologies of salvation and creation. But Gnosticism appears to be as rigidly male a religious system as Kabbalah, and one is therefore puzzled by the extraordinary interest in Gnosticism displayed by contemporary feminist theologians. The warning of Elizabeth Schuessler Fiorenza remains timely:

Salvation in the radically dualistic gnostic systems requires the annihilation and destruction of the female or the "feminine principle." In the moderately dualistic systems, salvation means the reunification of the male and female principle, while the male principle stands for the heavenly realms: Christ, God and Spirit. The female principle is secondary, since it stands for that part of the divine that became involved in the created world and history. Gnostic dualism shares in the patriarchal paradigm of Western culture. It makes the first principle male and defines femaleness relative to maleness. Maleness is the subject, the divine, the absolute; femaleness is the opposite or the complementary other.[59]

In Shi'ite Islam, mystical Judaism, and Gnostic Christianity there have been bold attempts to restore divine power to the first woman, producing so-called heretical Eves. But common themes run through such attempts, themes with which we are already familiar: a fear of the power of sexuality, and the need for women to fit into programs of male purification, male realization, male regeneration, and male restoration. The fascinating countertraditions of Western religion have led us into what looks to be a cul-de-sac. Is there a way out?

11. *Retrospect and Prospect: Eve and the Death of God*

For those feminists concerned with the religious dimensions of life, the absence of any spiritual tradition which resonates with their experience and which grounds women in a religious cosmos is one of the most insidious aspects of Western culture. To submit to the guidance of traditional religion is to become subjected to a kind of spiritual rape; to reject it is to fall prey to a powerful spiritual loneliness.[1]

It remains for us to summarize Eve's history and to imagine a future for her.

Eve's story begins with her death as a goddess and her rebirth as the first and representative woman. The procreating goddess of Near Eastern religions who, it is believed, cannot be trusted with religious power in a civilized society, is replaced in Genesis by Yahweh, the single, male deity who creates and acts. Eve becomes the daughter-wife of Adam, created to be his helper and to serve the designs of God through him. But a shadow falls over her from the moment of her creation. Less than Adam, not quite as much in the image of God as he, she becomes through her weaker nature the instrument of evil. She initiates the fall of humanity from paradisiacal communion with God and the earth into a world of toil, alienation, sex, reproduction, and death.

Through obedience to the covenant or the new Covenant, the possibility of forgiveness and redemption is offered to her, but that redemption is dependent on her acceptance of subjection to a man. Judaism and Christianity, with their theologies of marriage and the family, direct Eve to her duties of giving birth and raising children, and to serving the domestic needs of her husband. Roman Catholicism offers a second, higher calling as the virginal bride of Christ, the Second Eve.

Because Eve is seen as the one to blame for the fall of humanity, even her redeemed character is still viewed with suspicion, and special care must be taken to keep her under control. This view of her character is instructed not only by the Genesis story, but by the New Testament, the Talmud, the Qur'an and *hadith,* and Mariology, and by parts of the ancient pagan characterization of the Goddess, which are used to understand and flesh out those scriptures. Eve, and therefore feminine character in general, is regarded as less rational and less firmly in control of the passions, more gullible, more gifted in the arts of deception and persuasion, and more easily flattered into disloyalty.

Eve's sexuality is of special concern in the Western tradition. The Fall is regarded (whether literally or metaphorically) as a sexual event. Eve is guilty of wishing to be in control of her own sexual life. Some very deep, partially unarticulated fears are behind the male insistence that she be denied the freedom to make her own decisions about her bodily life. The notion of sexual renunciation, which is thrown into high relief by the Roman Catholic ideal of celibacy, is central to Christianity. As the Mother of All the Living, Eve has the power to deny life, and she must be convinced by religious and civil law that she cannot use this power. Therefore in Roman Catholicism the image of the obedient and dutiful Second Eve, the Virgin Mary, is held up to her, and in Protestantism the ideal of the Christian Mother is urged upon her.

Attempts to rework the myth of Eve so that lost religious powers are restored to her all fall victim to the old prejudices about the nature and destiny of Woman. The traditions that run alongside of, and at times counter to, those that have formed Western religion and civilization have, in the final analysis, been dominated by male concerns about the high cost, in psychological comfort and religious depth, of the "civilizing" image of the single, male deity. Some of Eve's lost power has been restored, and the necessity of regarding the Feminine as a part of the religious realm has been reaffirmed, but that restoration and reaffirmation has been largely inchoate, biased in its assessment of the negative attributes of the Mother Goddess, and directed toward meeting male needs.

Eve's history, then, has been a troubled one. What are the prospects for Eve's future?

✳

"Religious myths," Paula Landes writes, "appear to have a sort of life cycle. They emerge, they flourish, they wane. Eventually they die the death of unintelligibility or irrelevance once their relation to changing social circumstances can no longer be renegotiated through reinterpretation."[2] But the myth of Eve is neither unintelligible nor irrelevant. It remains deeply imbedded in both male and female ideas about the nature and destiny of women, and the attitudes it has engendered are embodied in the psychology, laws, religious life, and social structures of the Western world—not to mention the most intimate of human activities. Eve is very much alive, and every member of Western society is affected by her story.

Let us characterize four types of responses (with some overlap between them) to Eve's story. One group of people, those disinterested in what Landes calls the "religious dimensions of life," but concerned that men and women be free from what they see as the pernicious influence of an ideology, can strip the Eve myth of much of its continuing power over their lives by simply dismantling and scrutinizing the story to see how and why it came to be. The retelling of Eve's history can in this way enlighten and, having heightened the consciousness of its continued grip on Western attitudes toward women and its embodiment in Western institutions, help put an end to its negative influence.

Religious conservatives who maintain that, as troublesome as the provisions of the message might be, it is nonetheless God's Word will recognize that distinctions need to be made between the genuine message of the Scriptures and Church and cultural traditions that owe more to male prejudice and misunderstanding than to divine truth. The lives that religiously conservative women lead will not be independent or, in the fullest sense of the word, feminist. But with the understanding and support of sensitive husbands, their lives can be committedly Christian or Jewish, and characterized by joy, integrity, spiritual clarity, and love. We should remind ourselves at this point that American evangelicalism played a central role in the birth

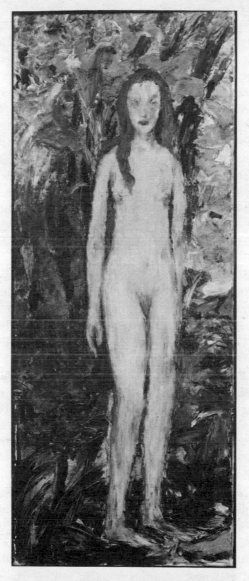

Eve, by Emil Nolde; 1910. Hagemann Collection, by permission of the Städelsches Museum, Frankfurt am Main, W. Germany.

and growth of modern feminism in the nineteenth century probably because at its heart is not religious, social, and political acculturation but a message that exists outside of group, nation, society, or political expression. From time to time, this message has reasserted itself with considerable force and impressive results. It could do so again.

A third response to the story of Eve may be characterized as liberal. If one believes that God's truth is always expressed in words and actions that are bound by time, place, and circumstance, then one can believe that God may speak new and liberating words that were not spoken in the past. The message may therefore be feminized if that is what a liberation theology calls for. The liberal believes that it is God's will that men and women be freed to be fully human, and any teaching, even biblical, that does not free us may be altered or rejected. Politically, this group struggles for changes in social and religious life that will provide genuine equality for women and is willing to experiment with sex roles. It is in the forefront of the efforts of women to gain control over their own bodies. Religiously, the liberal response calls for rewriting and reinterpreting the Bible, the liturgy, and Church doctrine—to root out sexist language and domination of the church by male clergy. This project must eventually come to terms with the fact that the language of Bible and Church doctrine is so closely bound up with the presupposition of a male deity that all pretension to reconstructing biblical or traditional theology must be given up. Liberals will discover, through the story of Eve, that feminism cannot effect reform, only revolution. As a group, therefore, it will have the greatest difficulty maintaining an identity, and there will be movement of members into other groups.

Feminism is the truly revolutionary movement of the twentieth century, because it cannot be reconciled with Western religion. This fact makes the fourth group of responses the most vital, interesting, and annoying. Having heard the story of Eve, and recognizing that to remain within traditional Western religion is to be, in Landes's words, "spiritually raped," they will attempt any and all combinations of old and new religious ideas in the search for a spiritual experience that resonates with what they have discovered to be true by themselves and for themselves. The religious groups thus engendered will be largely, by necessity or decree, exclusively female.

They will discover among themselves what they could not find in the company of men: new spiritual possibilities, new life possibilities, and new sexual possibilities. They, too will be involved in political and social change, often in ways that will prove too embarrassingly visible for the members of the first and third groups, which will provide most of the mass leadership of the women's movement.

It is this community that will have to exercise the most care that it does not find its expression in caricatured forms of some of the most tenacious and most vicious of male prejudices about women: their supposedly innate irrationality, subjectivism, emotionalism and vanity. What is essential is that their spiritual quest be genuinely free, and their own. But without a clear, guiding, "religious other" to which they are obedient, they could fall victim to various ideologized forms of self worship. That would be tragic, because it is from this group that we are likely to learn the most painful truth about ourselves and our possibilities.

I propose a new direction for the future of Eve. Chapter 1 began with the account of the death of the Goddess at the hands of the writers of Genesis, and her reappearance as a human woman upon whose character was superimposed the transparent image of her divine predecessor. It was suggested that the biblical creation story carries forward a religious revolution that began with the replacement of the Mother Goddess by the Father-God. The religion of the Old Testament legitimizes what is *not* religious—the secular order and man's activity in it—at the same time that it sets down rules for the extent, nature, and attitude of that order and activity. The Old Testament doctrine of God points away from God. Erich Fromm suggests[3] that what biblical theology requires of humanity is not really a theology at all, but "idology": the continual definition and rejection of idolatry, the worship of what is not God. The function of the doctrine of God is to check the pretensions to divinity of humans and their institutions.

The most characteristic response of religiously inclined feminists to the death of the Goddess has been to attempt to resuscitate her for the purposes of praise, inspiration, and emulation. Rejecting the claims of biblical theologians that the ancient Goddess was capricious, destructive, and incapable of providing a sustaining image for civilization, they have rediscovered and reasserted a pacifist Goddess who is only compassionate, wise, and healing. The realm over which this Goddess presided, and which feminists hope to recreate in their return to her, is seen as having been a seamless relationship between humans and nature, characterized by equality, gentleness, and love.

There is much to criticize in this vision. There is a notable lack of convincing evidence that there ever was a period of general worship of the Mother Goddess, let alone a correlated stage of equality between the sexes.[4] The modern characterization of the Goddess is more than a little tendentious and subjective, and its fascination with blood and soil seems reactionary to anyone who recalls twentieth-century German history. Man was reminded in the Old Testament that God was God and not Man, but feminists have not been ready to tell themselves that Goddess is Goddess and not Woman. To these criticisms, feminists reply that the Goddess image is indispensable; it frees women from the damaging image of the male God and provides the focal point for the construction of a nonsexist alternative religion.

One may ask, with D. L. Carmody, "whether the Goddess does not represent an intellectual regression, for all that she may represent an emotional advance."[5] One may also question whether gods and goddesses worthy of worship are recalled or created in just this way. But genuine spiritual questioning is in progress, and there is no compelling reason to reject the Goddess just yet. Eventually, however, feminist religion must converse with radical theology—the possibilities for religious thought opened up by the Death of God movement in the 1960s. Radical theology proposed that the reality to which the Bible directed humanity in worship and praise, and which addressed humanity in its successes and failures, was somehow gone. God is dead, and positive new religious possibilities, rather than catastrophe, follow this event.

It would appear that the two religious events are inseparable: The Death of God, and the Death of the Goddess. Since the history of Eve was so closely bound to the latter, the religious experience of women over several thousand years should tell us something about the former. If it is true that God is dead, Eve and feminism will still have much to teach us about the future possibilities of religion and our common life.

Notes

Chapter 1. The Mother of All the Living

1. Raphael Patai, *The Hebrew Goddess* (Philadelphia: KTAV, 1976), 15–16.
2. Isaac M. Kikawada, "Two Notes on Eve," *Journal of Biblical Literature* 91 (March 1972): 35.
3. Ibid., 34. See also Kate Millet, *Sexual Politics* (Garden City, N.J.: Doubleday, 1970), 52: ". . . The figure of Eve, like that of Pandora, has vestigial traces of a fertility goddess overthrown."
4. See Exod. 3:13–14.
5. Kikawada, "Two Notes on Eve," 35.
6. Alexander Heidel, *The Babylonian Genesis*, 2nd ed. (Chicago: University of Chicago Press, 1951). The text of *Enûma elish* is also included in James B. Pritchard, ed., *Ancient Near Eastern Texts Relating to the Old Testament*, 3rd ed. (Princeton: Princeton University Press, 1969).
7. Umberto Cassuto, *A Commentary on the Book of Genesis*, pt. 1 (Jerusalem: Magnes Press, Hebrew University, 1961), 7.
8. Heidel, *The Babylonian Genesis*, 98–101; Alfred Jeremias, *Das Alte Testament im Lichte des Alten Orients* (Leipzig, East Germany. J. C. Hinrichs, 1916), 36.
9. Elaine Pagels, "The Suppressed Gnostic Feminism," *The New York Review* 26, no. 18 (November 22, 1979): 42.
10. See Jer. 5:22; Ps. 104:7–9; Prov. 8:27–9; Job 7:12, 9:13, 26:10–12, 38:8–10; Isa. 27:1. See also Hermann Gunkel, *Schöpfung und Chaos in Urzeit und Endzeit* (Göttingen, West Germany: Vandenhoeck und Ruprecht, 1895); Robert Graves and Raphael Patai, *Hebrew Myths: The Book of Genesis* (New York: McGraw-Hill, 1964), 29–33; and Cassuto, *Commentary on Genesis*, 36–40.
11. Edmund Spenser, *The Faerie Queene*, cant. 1, lines 14–15.
12. Phyllis Trible, "Depatriarchalizing in Biblical Interpretation," in Elizabeth Koltun, ed., *The Jewish Woman: New Perspectives* (New York: Schocken Books, 1976), 217 ff.
13. Patai, *The Hebrew Goddess*, 21.
14. Ibid., 23–24.
15. Ludwig Köhler, *Old Testament Theology* (Philadelphia: Westminster Press, 1957), 69.
16. H. Wheeler Robinson, *Inspiration and Revelation in the Old Testament* (Oxford, England: Oxford University Press, 1946), 1.
17. Cassuto, *Commentary on the Book of Genesis*, 8.
18. Robinson, *Inspiration and Revelation in the Old Testament*, 4.
19. See Cassuto, *Commentary on the Book of Genesis*, 31 ff.
20. I am grateful to Carol Christ for this word.

21. See Erich Fromm, *You Shall Be As Gods* (New York: Holt, Rinehart and Winston, 1966).

22. Graves and Patai, *Hebrew Myths,* 40. See also Louis Ginzberg, *Legends of the Jews,* vol. 1 (1909; reprint, Philadelphia: Jewish Publication Society of America, 1937), 17–18 for a somewhat bowdlerized version. The original legend is from "Midrash Konen" in A. Jellinek, ed., *Bet Ha-Midrasch,* vol. 1 (Leipzig, East Germany: C. W. Vollrath, 1855).

23. Claus Westermann, *Beginning and End in the Bible* (Philadelphia: Westminster Press, 1972).

Chapter 2. Pandora: The Sorrow to Men Who Eat Bread

1. Geoffrey Ashe, *The Virgin* (London: Routledge and Kegan Paul, 1976), 17, 16.

2. See below, Chap. 4, 45–51.

3. See below, Chaps. 7 and 8.

4. Hesiod, *Works and Days and Theogony,* trans. Richard Lattimore (Ann Arbor, Mich.: University of Michigan Press, 1959), lines 57–58.

5. Hesiod, *Works and Days,* ed. H. G. Evelyn-White (Cambridge, Mass.: Harvard University Press, 1950), line 55.

6. Hesiod (Lattimore), "Theogony," *Works and Days and Theogony,* line 68.

7. Ibid., line 78.

8. Ibid., line 82.

9. Hesiod (Evelyn-White), *Works and Days,* lines 57–58.

10. Hesiod (Lattimore), "Theogony," *Works and Days and Theogony,* line 585.

11. Robert Graves, *The Greek Myths,* vol. 1 (New York: McGraw-Hill, 1955), 148; ibid., 2: 352.

12. See N. O. Brown, *Hermes the Thief: The Evolution of a Myth* (Madison, Wisc.: University of Wisconsin Press, 1947), 52 f. See also J. B. Russell, *The Devil* (Ithaca, N.Y.: Cornell University Press, 1977), 64.

13. Brown, *Hermes the Thief,* 52.

14. The various renderings of the myth are collected in Dora Panofsky and Erwin Panofsky, *Pandora's Box* (New York: Pantheon, 1962), 14–26.

15. Hesiod (Lattimore), "Works and Days," *Works and Days and Theogony,* lines 580–584.

16. Erich Neumann, *The Great Mother,* (Princeton, N.J.: Princeton University Press, 1963), 39–54. See also Wolfgang Lederer, *The Fear of Women* (New York: Harcourt, Brace, Jovanovich, 1970), 115–132.

17. Dora Panofsky and Erwin Panofsky, *Pandora's Box,* 49–51.

18. Jane E. Harrison, "Pandora's Box," in *Journal of Hellenic Studies* 20:108–109: "It is a quaint conflict of theological systems, and forasmuch as Zeus is omnipotent, he takes over even the creation of the Earth-Mother who was from the beginning; and patriarchal bourgeois as he is, the making of the first woman becomes a huge Olympian jest."

19. Hesiod (Lattimore), "Theogony," *Works and Days and Theogony,* line 590; "Works and Days," line 374.

20. Paul Schwarz, *Die Neue Eva* (Göppingen, West Germany: Kümmerle, 1973), 171.

21. Origen, "Contra Celsum" 4, in *The Ante-Nicene Fathers,* vol. 4 (Grand Rapids, Mich.: Eerdmans, 1956), 514.

22. Tertullian, "De corona militis" 7, *ibid.*, 3: 97. One can only speculate how much the Apologists found pagan pretensions amusing, and how much Hesiod's misogyny. Certainly Boccaccio, in his much later *Genealogy of the Pagan Gods*, counted on amusing males when he "misprinted" *Pandora* as *Pandorus* ("bitterness"), and then translated it as *omnium minus* ("lacking everything"), rather than *omnium munum* ("all gifts").

23. Quoted in Dora Panofsky and Erwin Panofsky, *Pandora's Box*, 12.

24. John Chrysostom, *In Mattheum homil*, xxxii, *ex capite* xix(a), Migne, *Patrologiae Graecae* vol. 56, 803.

25. Dora Panofsky and Erwin Panofsky, *Pandora's Box*, 15.

26. Ibid. In the sixteenth century, the humanist bishop Jean Oliver related Eve to Pandora with these words: "Eve in Scripture opened the forbidden fruit by her bite, by which death invaded the world. So did Pandora open the box in defiance of a divine injunction, whereby all the evils and infinite calamities broke loose and overwhelmed the hapless mortals with countless infirmities." (Quoted ibid., 155.)

27. Theodore Reik, *Myth and Guilt* (New York: G. Braziller, 1970), 64.

28. Ibid.

29. Dora Panofsky and Erwin Panofsky, *Pandora's Box*, 113.

Chapter 3. The Lady of the Rib

1. William McGuire, ed., *The Freud/Jung Letters* (Princeton, N.J.: Princeton University Press, 1974), 288 (Freud to Jung, December 17, 1911).

2. See below, Chap. 9.

3. Leo Steinberg, "The Line of Fate in Michelangelo's Painting," *Critical Inquiry* 6, no. 3 (Spring 1980): 439. Figure 29 depicts the diagonal line of fate that links the three portrayals of Eve.

4. The pairing of *'ish* with *'ishshah* is not as obvious as it would appear to an English-speaking reader, who would understand "man" and "woman" (literally, "wife of man") as truly related etymologically. The Hebrew words probably have only an assonantal connection, that is, they merely sound alike. See Bruce Vawter, *On Genesis* (New York: Doubleday, 1977), 75.

5. Thomas Aquinas, *Summa Theologiae* I.92.1.

6. See Ginzberg, *Legends of the Jews*, vol. 1 (1909; reprint, Philadelphia: Jewish Publication Society of America, 1937), 68.

7. Eph. 5:21 ff., Col. 3:18 ff.

8. Aquinas, *Summa Theologiae* I.92.1. This notion is clearly indebted to a midrash. See Ginzberg, *Legends of the Jews*, vol. 1, 66.

9. Augustine, *City of God* bk. 12, chap. 27.

10. Vawter, *On Genesis*, 65.

11. Graves and Patai, *Hebrew Myths*, 69, 15. Just as Boccaccio would later play with the name *Pandora*, and the authors of the *Malleus Malificarum* with *femina* (see below, pp. 70–72), one of the Latin Fathers, Hrabanus Maurus (ca. 775–855), mischievously translates "Eve" as *calamitas (De Universo viginti duo, lib.* II.1, in Migne, *Patrologiae Latinae* [hereafter *P.L.*], vol. v 91, 31).

12. The following quotations are from *Midrash Rabbah, Genesis I,* ed. H. Freedman and M. Simon (London: Soncino Press, 1939).

13. See also Ginzberg, *Legends of the Jews*, vol. 1, 64–65.

14. See also N. O. Brown, *Love's Body* (New York: Random House, 1966), 52.
15. Philo Judaeus, *de Opificio Mundi,* in F. H. Colson and G. H. Whitaker, trans., *Philo,* vol. 1 (Cambridge, Mass.: Harvard University Press, 1929), 119–120.
16. *Yebamoth,* verse 63a (Aramaic), in M. L. Rodkinson, trans., *The Talmud* (New York: New Amsterdam Book Co., 1903).
17. See Num. 32:38; 2 Kings 23:24, 24:17 and 2 Chron. 36:4; also Cassuto, *A Commentary on the Book of Genesis,* 130, 170; and Trible, "Depatriarchalizing in Biblical Interpretation," 217 ff.
18. Mary Daly, *Beyond God the Father* (Boston: Beacon Press, 1973), 45.
19. Geza Roheim points out that the story of Eve's creation concludes with the naming scene in the same way that the encounter with the snake concludes with the cursing scene; that is, the naming is meant to be seen as a punishment—Adam's assertion of dominance over the woman. "The Garden of Eden," *Psychoanalytic Review,* 27, no. 1 (January 1940): 1–26; ibid., no. 2 (April 1940): 177–199.
20. See Trible, "Depatriarchalizing in Biblical Interpretation," 223.
21. Dracontius, *Carmen de deo* bk. 1, lines 393–397, in *P.L.,* vol. 50, 729–730.
22. John Milton, *Paradise Lost* bk. 7, verses 1183–1191.
23. Ibid. bk. i, verses 537–546.
24. Aquinas, *Summa Theologiae* 1a.92, i.
25. Ibid. See Aristotle, *de Generatione Animalium* IV.2, 766b33.
26. John Milton, *Paradise Lost* bk. 9, verses 532, 533, 538, 568, 612, 732, 547–548.
27. C. A. Patrides, *Milton and the Christian Tradition* (Oxford, England: Oxford University Press, 1966), 105.
28. J. Calvin, *Commentary on Genesis* (Grand Rapids, Mich.: Eerdmans, 1948), bk. lx, 999.
29. See Graves and Patai, *Hebrew Myths,* 60–62; Philo Judaeus, *de Opificio Mundi,* 24, 46, 51; Ginzberg, *Legends of the Jews* 1:49–62; ibid., 5:63–64, 5:71–73, 5:79–80.

Chapter 4. The Serpent-Mother

1. Hugo Gressmann, "Mythische Reste in der Paradieserzählung," in *Archiv für Religionswissenschaft,* vol. 10 (Leipzig, East Germany, 1907), 358. Compare Cassuto, *A Commentary on the Book of Genesis,* 142.
2. R. Graves and R. Patai, *Hebrew Myths: The Book of Genesis* (New York: McGraw-Hill, 1964), 65 ff.
3. Freeman and M. Simon, eds., *Midrash Rabbah, Genesis I* (London: Soncino Press, 1935), xvii.7; Ginzberg, *Legends of the Jews,* vol. 1, 68.
4. H. Freedman and M. Simon, eds., *Midrash Rabbah, Genesis I,* XVIII.4.
5. For what follows, see Ginzberg, *Legends of the Jews,* vol. 1, (1909; reprint, Philadelphia: Jewish Publication Society of America, 1937), 65–66; ibid., 5:86, ln. 38; 5:87-88, ln. 40; and 5:147-148; Graves and Patai, *Hebrew Myths,* 65–66; A. S. Rappoport and R. Patai, *Myth and Legend in Ancient Israel,* vol. I (Philadelphia: KTAV, 1966), 77–79; Gershom Scholem, "Lilith," in Cecil Roth, ed., *Encyclopedia Judaica* (New York: Macmillan, 1971), vol. 11; Raphael Patai, *The Hebrew Goddess* (Philadelphia: KTAV, 1976), 207–245.
6. With the exception of Isa. 34:14-15, where she is said to inhabit desert wastes, Lilith has been completely exorcised from Scripture.

7. Dante, *Purgatorio* Cant. 19, versus 58–59.

8. Aviva Cantor Zuckoff, "The Lilith Question," *Lilith* 1, no. 2 (Fall 1976): 5 ff., 10.

9. Patai, *The Hebrew Goddess, passim.*

10. See Bruce Vawter, *On Genesis* (New York: Doubleday, 1977), 86–87.

11. Ibid.

12. Graves and Patai, *Hebrew Myths,* 69.

13. T. H. Gaster, *Myth, Legend and Custom in the Old Testament* (New York: Harper & Row, 1969), 36. See also Graves and Patai, *Hebrew Myths,* 80.

14. Paul Schwarz, *Die Neue Eva* (Göppingen, West Germany: Kümmerle), 61.

15. Ibid.

16. Hans Sachs, "Schwank, der Hundesschwantz," in Adelbert von Keller, ed., *Hans Sachs Werke,* vol. 9 (Stuttgart, West Germany: A. Hiersemann, 1964), 304–305. This story is probably the origin of the vulgar English expression for women, "piece of tail." The word *Schwantz* in German means either "tail" or "penis."

17. Schwarz, *Die Neue Eva,* 62.

18. R. H. Charles, ed. and trans. *The Apocrypha and Pseudepigrapha of the Old Testament,* vol. 2 (Oxford: Clarendon Press, 1913).

19. *Guthlac,* lines 980-985, quoted in J. M. Evans, *Paradise Lost and the Genesis Tradition* (Oxford, England: Oxford University Press, 1968), 149.

20. *Acta Archelai,* chap. 10, quoted ibid., 66–72. A similar tradition is recorded in the Babylonian Talmud: "Rabbi Johanan stated: when the serpent copulated with Eve, he infused her with lust," Yebamoth, verse 103a, in M. L. Rodkinson, trans., *The Talmud* (New York: New Amsterdam Book Co., 1903). Both *Midrash Rabbah, Genesis I* (H. Freedman and M. Simon, eds., XVIII.6) and Rashi, in *Pentateuch and Rashi's Commentary on Genesis,* iii,I, tr. M. Rosenbaum and A. M. Silberman, vol. 1 (Genesis) (London: Routledge and Kegan Paul 1929), 13, repeat the story that the serpent contemplated marriage with Eve.

22. Quoted in Theodore Reik, *Myth and Guilt* (New York: G. Braziller, 1970), 113–114.

23. "For the ego and the male, the female is synonymous with the unconscious and the nonego, hence with darkness, nothingness, the void, the bottomless pit. Mother, womb, the pit and hell are all identical. The womb of the female is the place of origin from whence one came, and so every female . . . threatens the ego with the danger of self-naughting, of self-loss—in other words, with death and castration." Erich Neumann, *The Great Mother* (Princeton, N.J.: Princeton University Press, 1963), 157–158). See chap. 6,.

24. The subtle wordplay of the Yahwist is important. In the last verse of Gen. 2, the couple is described as being "naked" *(arummim).* The serpent is then introduced in the first verse of Chapter 3, and he is characterized by his "shrewdness" or "cleverness" *(arumim).* Eve's attentiveness to his words leads to the couple's consciousness of their nakedness.

25. Vawter, *On Genesis,* 79.

26. Reik, *Myth and Guilt,* 113–114.

27. For what follows, see N. P. Williams, *Ideas of the Fall and Original Sin* (London: Longmans, Green and Co., 1927).

28. For the texts of the following intertestamental writings, see R. H. Charles, *Apocrypha and Pseudepigrapha,* vol. 1; ibid., vol. 2.

29. Milton was certainly acquainted with the tradition that the sons of God were actually seduced. See *Paradise Lost,* verses 620–627.

30. Ginzberg paraphrases the story in *Legends of the Jews,* vol. 1, 94–98.

31. See below, 124.

32. Philo Judaeus, *Hypothetica,* chap. 11, verses 14–17, in F. H. Colson and G. H. Whitaker, trans., *Philo,* vol. 10 (Cambridge, Mass.: Harvard University Press, 1929).

Chapter 5. The Devil's Gateway

1. Heinrich Kramer and James Sprenger, *Malleus Maleficarum,* 1486? trans. and intro. by Montague Summers, (London: Pushkin Press, 1951), 47.

2. Bruce Vawter, *On Genesis* (New York: Doubleday 1977), p. 79.

3. Mary Daly, *Beyond God the Father* (Boston: Beacon Press, 1973), 45.

4. See below, chaps. 3 and 4.

5. Dracontius, quoted in J. M. Evans, *Paradise Lost and the Genesis Tradition* (Oxford, England: Oxford University Press, 1968), 32; Cyril of Jerusalem, *Catechetical Lectures,* xii.5, in E. H. Gifford, ed., *A Select Library of the Nicene and Post-Nicene Fathers,* vol. 7, (Grand Rapids: Eerdmans, 1958); Augustine, *City of God,* bk. 14, chap. 2; Martin Luther, *Lectures on Genesis, Chaps. 1–5 in J. Pelikan, ed., Luther's Works,* vol. 1 (St. Louis, Mo.: Concordia, 1958), 151.

6. Luther, *Lectures on Genesis,* chaps. 1–5, 151.

7. Paul Schwarz, *Die Neue Eve* (Göppingen, West Germany: Kümmerle, 1973), 168–169.

8. Eric Auerbach, *Mimesis* (Princeton, N.J.: Princeton University Press, 1953), 147, 150–151.

9. Peter Comestor, quoted in J. M. Evans, *Paradise Lost and the Genesis Tradition,* 170–171.

10. Augustine, *Genesis ad. lit.,* xi.xxx, quoted in ibid., 97; Thomas Aquinas, *Summa Theologiae* II.clxiii.4.

11. P. Studer, ed., *Mystère d'Adam* (Manchester, England: University Press, 1918), lines 253–255.

12. *Poematum de Mosaicae Historiae Gestis,* quoted in Evans, *Paradise Lost and the Genesis Tradition,* 135–136

13. Dante, *Purgatorio,* Cant. 24, verse 115; *Paradiso,* cant., 13 verse 37.

14. Gerhard von Rad, *Genesis* (Philadelphia: Westminster Press, 1971), 87–88.

15. Cassuto, *A Commentary on the Book of Genesis,* pt. 1 (Jerusalem: Magnes Press, Hebrew University 1961), 147.

16. Philo Judaeus, *de Opificio Mundi,* in F. H. Colson and G. H. Whitaker, trans., *Philo,* vol. 1 (Cambridge, Mass: Harvard University Press 1929), 111–112.

17. Cassuto, *A Commentary on the Book of Genesis,* 140, 160.

18. Ibid., 142–143, 147.

19. Peter Comestor, *Historia Scholastica: Liber Genesis,* in *P.L.,* vol. 198, col. 1072.

20. J. K. Bonnell, "The Serpent with a Human Head in Art and in Mystery Play," *American Journal of Archaeology* 21 (1917): 255 ff.

21. John Chrysostom, *Homiliae in Genesium,* quoted in Evans, *Paradise Lost and the Genesis Tradition,* 88.

22. Gregory of Nyssa, *On the Baptism of Christ,* in E. H. Gifford, ed., *Select Library of the Nicene and Post-Nicene Fathers,* vol. 5, 519.

23. Augustine, *City of God* bk. 14, chap. 2.
24. Ginzberg, *Legends of the Jews,* vol. 1 (1909; reprint, Philadelphia: Jewish Publication Society of America, 1937), 96. See also ibid. vol. 5, 133, note 3.
25. Charles de Tolnay, *Michelangelo,* vol. 2, (Princeton: Princeton University Press, 1945), 31.
26. Leo Steinberg, "A Corner of the Last Judgement," *Daedelus* 109, no. 2 (Spring 1980): 207–273.
27. Elizabeth Katsivelos, quoted in Leo Steinberg, "Eve's Idle Hand," *Art Journal* 35, no. 2 (Winter 1975/6), 131. See also Leo Steinberg, "The Line of Fate in Michelangelo's Painting," *Critical Inquiry* 6, no. 3 (Spring 1980): 441.
28. Kramer and Sprenger, *Malleus Maleficarum,* 43.
29. Ibid., 43, 44.
30. Ibid., 46, 47.
31. Ibid., 47.
32. John Milton, *Christian Doctrine,* in *Complete Prose Works of John Milton,* vol. 6 (New Haven, Conn.: Yale University Press, 1973), 383.
33. Robert Lowell, "Epics," *The New York Review, of Books* 27, no. 2 (October 23, 1977): 3–6.
34. "Calculated lying": John Milton, *Paradise Lost,* bk. 9, verses 827–833; "marital faith": Grotius, *Adamus Exul,* quoted in Evans, *Paradise Lost and the Genesis Tradition,* 210; "impugning his courage": *Poematum de Mosaicae Historiae Gestis,* quoted ibid., 137, and *Mystere d'Adam,* quoted ibid., 202; "moves his heart": Proba, quoted ibid., 118; "reasons": Grotius, *Adamus Exul,* quoted ibid., 211; "pleading and persuading": Chrysostom, quoted ibid., 91, and Comestor, quoted ibid., 171; "deceiving": *Pirke Rabbi Eliezer,* quoted ibid., 203, and *The Chester Plays,* quoted ibid., 203; "appeals to sentiment": H. Freedman and M. Simon, eds., *Midrash Rabbah, Genesis 1* (London: Soncino Press 1935), xix.5.
35. A medieval Armenian Gnostic tale, quoted in Schwarz, *Die Neue Eva,* 47.
36. Cassuto, *Commentary on Genesis,* 148 (my italics).
37. Schwarz, *Die Neue Eva,* 51.
38. Ibid., 38. See also Jubilees 3:7 (in R. H. Charles, ed. and trans, *Apocrypha and Pseudepigrapha of the Old Testament* [Oxford, England: Clarendon Press, 1913], vol. 2) which holds that Adam was tempted for seven years.
39. Augustine, *City of God* bk. 14, chap. 11.
40. Thomas Aquinas, *Summa Theologiae* II.clxiii.4.
41. *Mirk's Festial,* quoted in J. M. Evans, *Paradise Lost and the Genesis Tradition,* 180; *Speculum Humanae Salvationis,* quoted ibid., 181; *Chasteau d'Amour,* quoted ibid., 180.
42. Tertullian, "On the Apparel of Women," in *The Ante-Nicene Fathers,* vol. 4 (Grand Rapids, Mich.: Eerdmans, 1956), 14.
43. J. Calvin, *Commentary on Genesis* (Grand Rapids, Mich.: Eerdmans, 1948), bk. 2, 18.
44. Theodore Reik, *Myth and Guilt* (New York: G. Braziller, 1970), 110.
45. Comestor, quoted in J. M. Evans, *Paradise Lost and the Genesis Tradition,* 172.
46. Vincent of Beauvais, quoted ibid., 178–179. Ginzberg records the tradition that Eve's first menstruation coincided with the eating of the forbidden fruit—therefore, quite properly, "the Curse" (*Legends of the Jews,* vol. 5, 101, n. 85). "The verdict against Eve also consisted in ten curses, the effect of which is

184 EVE: THE HISTORY OF AN IDEA

noticeable to this day in the physical, spiritual and social state of women (ibid, vol. 1, 78)."
47. Thomas Aquinas, *Summa Theologiae* II.clxiii.4.
48. Indeed, for all nature. She is said in a *midrash* to have completed the Fall by giving the fruit to all of the animals in turn (see L. Ginzberg, *Legends of the Jews* vol. 1, 74.
49. David Greene and Frank Connor, eds. and trans., *A Golden Treasury of Irish Poetry, 600–1200* (London: Macmillan, 1967), 158.

Chapter 6. "Mother Incest So Familiar to Us"

1. The *Exsultet* from the liturgy for Holy Saturday.
2. J. C. F. Schiller, "Thalia," in Karl-Heinz Hahn, ed., *Schillers Werke,* vol. 17 (Weimar, East Germany: Aufbau-Verlag, 1970) 398–413.
3. "Adam Lay Ybounden," Percy Dearmer, ed., *The Oxford Book of Carols* (London: Oxford University Press, 1961), 386–388.
4. Moses Maimonides, *Guide of the Perplexed,* trans. and intro. by Schlomo Pines (Chicago: University of Chicago Press, 1963), 23–24.
5. J. B. Russell, *Satan: The Early Christian Tradition* (Ithaca, N.Y.: Cornell University Press, 1981), 83.
6. Irenaeus, "Irenaeus Against Heresies," bk. ii, in *The Ante-Nicene Fathers,* vol. 1 (Grand Rapids, Mich.: Eerdmans, 1956), 365.
7. *Libellus,* bk x, verses 8b–9a, in Walter Scott, trans., *Hermetica,* vol. 1 (Oxford, England: Clarendon Press 1924), 193.
8. Schiller, "Thalia," 398–9.
9. Julius Wellhausen, *Prolegomena to the History of Israel,* J. S. Black and A., Menzies, trans. (Edinburgh, Scotland: A. and C. Black, 1885). Hermann Gunkel, the father of modern Genesis criticism, regarded the Fall story as a straightforward etiology that accounted for adult knowledge of sexual matters of which children are innocent. See Hermann Gunkel, *Genesis* (Göttingen, West Germany: Vanderhoeck und Ruprecht 1910), and Hermann Gunkel, *Legends of Genesis,* W. H. Carruth, trans. (Chicago: The Open Court Publishing Co., 1907).
10. August Dillmann, *Genesis Critically and Exegetically Expounded,* trans. W. B. Stevenson (Edinburgh, Scotland: T and T Clark, 1897), 146.
11. Hugo Gressmann, "Paradis und Sunde," *Die Christliche Welt* 26 (1926): 844.
12. Claus Westermann, *Genesis 1–12* (Darmstadt, West Germany: Wissenschaftliche Buchgesellschaft, 1972), 92.
13. Schwarz, *Die Neue Eva* (Göppingen, West Germany: Kümmerle, 1973), 7–8.
14. Ibid., 17.
15. Ibid.
16. Ibid., 31.
17. Erich Neumann, *The Great Mother* (Princeton, N.J.: Princeton University Press, 1963), 214–215.
18. Ibid., 12.
19. Erich Neumann, *The Origins and History of Consciousness* (Princeton, N.J.: Princeton University Press, 1954), 158.
20. Sigmund Freud, *Moses and Monotheism* (New York: Knopf, 1939).
21. William McGuire, ed., *The Freud/Jung Letters* (Princeton, N.J.: Princeton University Press, 1974), 288.

22. Geza Roheim, "The Garden of Eden," *Psychoanalytic Review* 27, no. 1 (January, 1940): 1–26; ibid., no. 2 (April, 1940): 177–199.

23. Ibid., 2.

24. Ludwig Levy, "Sexualsymbolik in der biblischen Paradisgeschichte," *Imago* 1 (1917; reprint 1969 as vol. 5, 1917–1919): 19.

25. Geza Roheim, "The Garden of Eden," *Psychoanalytic Review* 27, no. 2: 178.

26. Ibid., 199.

27. Erich Fromm, *You Shall Be As Gods* (New York: Holt, Rinehart and Winston, 1966), 70–71, 87–88.

28. Geza Roheim, "The Garden of Eden," *Psychoanalytic Review* 27, no. 2: 178.

29. Wolfgang Lederer, *The Fear of Women* (New York: Harcourt, Brace, Jovanovich, 1968); Andrea Dworkin, *Woman Hating* (New York: Dutton, 1974).

Chapter 7. "A Nail Driven Into the Wall"

1. Karl Barth, *Church Dogmatics* (Edinburgh, Scotland: T. and T. Clark, 1955 f.), 3/2, 287.

2. Martin Luther, *Lectures on Genesis, Chaps. 1–5,* in J. Pelikan, ed., *Luther's Works,* vol. 1 (St. Louis, Mo: Concordia, 1958), 69, 115.

3. John Calvin, *Commentary on Genesis* (Grand Rapids, Mich.: Eerdmans, 1948), bk ii.9.

4. Ibid.

5. Ibid.

6. Milton, *Paradise Lost,* bk. 4, 299.

7. Ibid., bk. 8, 232–233.

8. Ibid.

9. Ibid., bk. 8, 816–825.

10. J. M. Evans, *Paradise Lost and the Genesis Tradition* (Oxford, England: Oxford University Press, 1968), 275.

11. Northrop Frye, *The Return of Eden* (Toronto, Canada: University of Toronto Press, 1965), 77. Feminist theologian Phyllis Trible makes the same point: "There is no consultation with her husband. She seeks neither his advice nor his permission. She acts independently." "Depatriarchalizing in Biblical Interpretation," in Elizabeth Koltun, ed., *The Jewish Woman: New Perspectives* (New York: Schocken Books, 1976), 226.

12. A. Fowler in J. Carey and A. Fowler, eds., *The Poems of John Milton* (London: Longmans, 1968), 869 n.

13. See Edward Le Comte, *Milton and Sex* (New York: Columbia University Press, 1978).

14. John Milton, *Paradise Lost,* bk. 9, lines 1155–1156.

15. Ibid., bk. 8, lines 1182–1184.

16. John Milton, *Christian Doctrine,* in *Complete Prose Works of John Milton,* vol. 6 (New Haven, Conn.: Yale University Press, 1973), 383.

17. J. Calvin, *Commentary on Genesis,* chap. 2, verse 18. ii. 18.

18. M. Luther, *Lectures on Genesis,* 69, 115.

19. Ibid., 116, 202–203.

20. J. Milton, *Christian Doctrine,* 383.

21. J. Calvin, *Commentary on Genesis* chap. 2, verse 18.

22. Gregory of Nazianzus, "On the Death of His Father," *Select Library of the Nicene and Post-Nicene Fathers,* vol. 7, 256–257.
23. Karl Barth, *Church Dogmatics,* 1/3, 195, 288, 289–290.
24. Ibid., 3/4, 156. Barth would have applauded the remark made by someone in another context: "God created Adam and Eve, not Adam and Bruce."
25. Ibid., 1/3, 295 (italics mine).
26. Ibid., 169.
27. Elizabeth Clark and Herbert Richardson, eds., *Women and Religion* (New York: Harper & Row, 1977), 239–258.
28. Trible, Phyllis "Depatriarchalizing in Biblical Interpretation," 223.
29. Karl Barth, *Church Dogmatics,* 3/2, 287.
30. Ibid., 3/4, 151.
31. Ibid., 170.
32. Ibid., 170–171.
33. Ibid., 3/2, 287.
34. Ibid., 3/4, 168.
35. Ibid., 172.
36. Claus Westermann, *Genesis,* 1–12 (Darmstadt, West Germany: Wissenschaftliche Buchgesellschaft, 1972), 357–358.
37. Ibid., 357.
38. Ibid., 358.
39. Graves and R. Patai, *Hebrew Myths: The Book of Genesis* (New York: McGraw-Hill, 1964), 69.
40. *De Mosaicae Historiae,* chap. iii, lines 105–107, quoted in J. M. Evans, *Paradise Lost and the Genesis Tradition* (Oxford, England: Oxford University Press, 1968), 137; *Mystère d'Adam,* 357–364, quoted ibid., 204.
41. Mary Daly, *Beyond God the Father* (Boston: Beacon Press, 1973), 62.

Chapter 8. The "Eschatological Woman"

1. Dante, *Purgatorio,* cant. 29, verses 24–30.
2. Robin Scroggs, *The Last Adam* (Philadelphia: Fortress, 1967).
3. "Paul and the Eschatological Woman," in *Journal of the American Academy of Religion* 40, no. 3 (September 1972): 283–303. See also "Paul and the Eschatological Woman Revisited," and Elaine Pagels, "Paul and Women: A Response to Recent Discussion," ibid., 42, no. 3 (September 1974): 532–540.
4. See also William O. Walker, Jr., "I Corinthians 11:2–16 and Paul's Views Regarding Women," *Journal of Biblical Literature* 94, no. 1 (March 1975): 94–110.
5. R. Scroggs, "Paul and the Eschatological Woman," 283.
6. Ibid., 302.
7. Ibid., 284.
8. Ginzberg records evidence for such a custom among Jews: "Woman covers her hair in token of Eve's having brought sin into the world; she tires to hide her shame" (Louis Ginzberg, *Legends of the Jews,* vol. 1 [1909; reprint, Philadelphia: Jewish Publication Society of America, 1937], 67). See also ibid., n. 45). We have also the *midrash:* "Why does a . . . woman go out with her head covered? She is like one who has done wrong and is ashamed of people; therefore she goes out with her head covered," H. Freedman and M. Simon, eds., *Midrash Rabba: Genesis I* (London: Soncino Press, 1939), xvii.
9. Tertullian, *Adversus Marcionem,* bk. chap. 8, in *P. L.,* vol. 2, 520. See the

development of the "Watchers" tradition, above, 45–51.

10. "The Sophia of Jesus Christ," 118:15–17, in J. M. Robinson, ed., *The Nag Hammadi Library in English* (San Francisco: Harper & Row, 1977), 206–228. See also G. W. MacRae, "The Jewish Background of the Gnostic Sophia Myth," *Novum Testamentum* 12 (1969): 100.

11. C. K. Barrett, *A Commentary on the First Epistle to the Corinthians* (New York: Harper & Row, 1968), 250–257.

12. Elizabeth Cady Stanton, *The Women's Bible* (c. 1895–1898; reprint Seattle, Wash.: Coalition Task Force on Women and Religion, 1974).

13. Ibid., 7, 8, 12.

Chapter 9. The Second Eve

1. Leo Steinberg, "The Line of Fate in Michelangelo's Painting," *Critical Inquiry* 6, no. 3 (Spring 1980): 437–439.

2. Luke 1:26–56. See John de Satgé, *Mary and the Christian Gospel* (London: SPCK, 1976).

3. Justin Martyr, *Dialogue with Trypho,* trans. A. L. Williams, chap., verse 5 (London: SPCK, 1930), 21.

4. Irenaeus, quoted by de Satgé, *Mary and the Christian Gospel,* 120.

5. Tertullian, *de carne Christi* chap. 17, *P.L.,* vol. 2, 781–782.

6. Jerome, "Letter 22 to Eustachius: The Virgin's Profession," F. A. Wright, trans, *Select Letters of St. Jerome* (Cambridge, Mass.: Harvard University Press, 1933), 60.

7. Marina Warner, *Alone of All Her Sex* (New York: Knopf, 1976), 49.

8. Bernard of Clairvaux, *Super Missus est Homiliae, Hom.* 2, part 3, *P.L.* vol. 183, pt. 2, 62.

9. Albertus Magnus, quoted in John de Satgé, *Mary and the Christian Gospel,* 128.

10. Marina Warner, *Alone of All Her Sex* (New York: Knopf, 1976), 73.

11. See Hilda Graef, *Mary: A History of Doctrine and Devotion* (New York: Seed and Ward, 1964).

12. Marina Warner, *Alone of All Her Sex,* 251.

13. R. E. Brown et al., *Mary in the New Testament* (Philadelphia: Fortress Press, 1978), 228–229.

14. Giovanni Mieggi, *The Virgin Mary,* Philadelphia: Westminster Press, 1955), 102. See John Sweet, *Revelation* (Philadelphia: Westminster Press, 1979), and J. M. Ford, *Revelation* (New York: Doubleday, 1975).

15. Karl J. von Hefele, *History of the Christian Councils,* trans. and ed. W. R. Clark (Edinburgh, Scotland: T. and T. Clark, 1871), 233 f.

16. Geoffrey Ashe, *The Virgin* (London: Routledge and Kegan Paul, 1976), 122.

17. Another tendency, undeveloped in Roman Catholicism, became a primary concern for the Eastern church: the relationship between the Virgin Mary and *Sophia,* the Creative Wisdom: "In [the Virgin] is realized the idea of Divine Wisdom in the creation of the world; she is Divine Wisdom in the created world. . . . Living in heaven in a state of glory the Virgin remains the mother of the human race. . . . She covers the world with her veil" (Sergei Bulgakov, *The Orthodox Church* [London: Centenary Press, 1935], 139).

18. Marina Warner, *Alone of All Her Sex,* 59.

19. Raphael Patai, *The Hebrew Goddess* (Philadelphia: KTAV, 1976), 192.

20. Ibid., 187, 190, 203. Patai misses the change in the ancient doctrine brought about by Mariology.

188 EVE: THE HISTORY OF AN IDEA

21. Marina Warner, *Alone of All Her Sex,* 93.
22. Dante, *Purgatorio,* cant. xix.
23. Shakespeare, *King Lear,* act IV, sc. 6.
24. Warner, *Alone of All Her Sex,* 73–74.
25. Ibid., 60
26. Ibid., 336.
27. Jerome, *Comm. in Epist. ad Ephes.,* III.5, quoted in Mary Daly, *The Church and the Second Sex* (New York: Harper and Row, 1968) 43. See also Ambrose, quoted in Marina Warner, *Alone of All Her Sex,* 73.
28. Marina Warner, *Alone of All Her Sex,* 67.
29. Ibid., 338.
30. Daly, *The Church and the Second Sex,* 81, 62.

Chapter 10. The Countertradition: Heretical Eves

1. "On the Origins of the Word," 115:31–116:8, in J. M. Robinson, ed., *The Nag Hammadi Library in English* (San Francisco: Harper & Row, 1977), 172.
2. "The Book of Government, or Rules for Kings" (trans. London, 1960), in J. A. Williams, ed., *Themes of Islamic Civilization* (Berkeley, Calif.: University of California Press, 1971) 9–11.
3. Paul Schwarz, *Die Neue Eva* (Göppingen, West Germany: Kümmerle, 1973), 34.
4. Ignaz Goldziher, *Muslim Studies,* vol. 2 (London: Allen and Irwin, 1967), 271.
5. See Geoffrey Parrinder, *Jesus in the Qur'an* (London: Oxford University Press, 1977).
6. Syed Ameer Ali, "Fatima," H. A. R. Gibb and J. H. Kramers, eds., *A Shorter Encyclopedia of Islam* (Leiden: E. J. Brill, 1953), 101.
7. L. Vecchia Vaglieri, "Fatima," in *The Encyclopedia of Islam,* new ed., B. Lewis, C. Pellat and J. Schacht, eds. (London: Luzac & Co., 1960), Ch. 2: 841–850.
8. Frithjof Schuon, *Dimensions of Islam* (London: Allen and Union, 1969), 126.
9. Fatima Mernissi, *Beyond the Veil* (Cambridge, Mass: Schenkman Publishing Co., 1975), 1–13.
10. Ibid., 2.
11. Ibid., 4.
12. Ibid., 5.
13. Mernissi records two of many Muslim sayings relating women to *fitna:* "She resembles Satan in his irresistible power over the individual" (Abu al-Hassan); and "[Muhammad] said: 'After my disappearance there will be no greater source of chaos and disorder for my nation than women" (al-Bukhari). Ibid., 11, 13.
14. R. Patai, *Hebrew Goddess* (Philadelphia: KTAV, 1976).
15. For what follows, see ibid. and Gershom Scholem, *Major Trends in Jewish Mysticism* (New York: Schocken, 1954), 225–239.
16. G. Scholem, *Major Trends in Jewish Mysticism,* 230.
17. Ibid., 276.
18. Ibid., 230.
19. Ibid., 232.
20. Ibid.
21. R. Patai, *Hebrew Goddess,* 191.

22. Ibid.
23. G. Scholem, *Major Trends in Jewish Mysticism,* 233.
24. R. Patai, *Hebrew Goddess,* 195–196.
25. G. Scholem, *Major Trends in Jewish Mysticism,* 235.
26. Ibid., 232.
27. Ibid., 37–38.
28. Ibid.
29. Ibid.
30. Irenaeus, "Irenaeus Against Heresies," bk. 3, chap. 15; bk. 4, chap. 26; bk. 1, chap. 27; in *The Anti-Nicene Fathers,* vol. 1 (Grand Rapids, Mich.: Eerdmans, 1956).
31. See for what follows Werner Foerster, *Gnosis* (Oxford, England: Clarendon Press, 1972).
32. J. M. Robinson, ed., *The Nag Hammadi Library in English,* passim.
33. Robert M. Grant, ed., *Gnosticism* (New York: Harper & Row, 1961), 94–100.
34. Ibid., 180–187.
35. Ibid., 52–59.
36. J. M. Robinson, ed., *The Nag Hammadi Library in English,* 329–338.
37. Ibid., 112.
38. G. C. Stead, "The Valentinian Myth of Sophia," *Journal of Theological Studies* 20, part 1 (April 1969): 75–104.
39. G. W. MacRae, "The Jewish Background of the Gnostic Sophia Myth," *Novum Testamentum* 12 (1969).
40. Ibid., 99–100.
41. Institute for Antiquity and Christianity, *The Nag Hammadi Library in English,* 101.
42. Ibid., 172–173.
43. Ibid., 161–179.
44. Ibid., 271–272.
45. G. C. Stead, "The Valentinian Myth of Sophia", 104.
46. See B. A. Pearson, "Jewish Haggadic Tradition in the Theology of Truth from Nag Hammadi C. G. IX, 3," *Ex Orbe Religionem* (Leiden: E. J. Brill, 1972), 453–470.
47. Elaine Pagels, *The Gnostic Gospels* (New York: Random House, 1977).
48. J. M. Robinson, ed., *The Nag Hammadi Library in English,* 438.
49. Ibid., 180–187.
50. Ibid., 130.
51. *Zostrianos* in Ibid., 393.
52. *Dialogue of the Savior,* ibid. 237.
53. See 2 Clement of Alexandria, *Stromata* III, ix, in M. R. James, *The Apocryphal New Testament* (Oxford, England: Clarendon Press, 1924), 10–11; *The Apocalypse of Adam,* in J. M. Robinson, ed., *The Nag Hammadi Library in English,* 256–257; John Bugge, *Virginitas: An Essay in the History of a Medieval Ideal* (The Hague, Netherlands: Martinus Nijhoff, 1975), 19.
54. J. M. Robinson, ed., *The Nag Hammadi Library in English,* 141, 142.
55. Ibid., 149
56. J. Bugge, *Virginitas: An Essay in the History of a Medieval Ideal,* 12.
57. Epiphanius, *Exposition fidei catholicae,* bk. xxi, in *P.G..* vol. 42, 823–824. In his *History of Dogma,* Harnack writes: "Protestants at the present day can hardly

form a conception of the hold which asceticism possessed over the mind of the fourth and fifth centuries, or of the manner in which it influenced imagination, thought and the whole of life. At bottom, only a single point was dealt with, abstinence from sexual relationships; everything else was secondary. . . . Virginity was the specifically Christian virtue: in this conviction the meaning of the evangelical law was summed up" (Adolf von Harnack, *History of Dogma,* vol. 3, trans. Neil Buchanan, (New York: Dover, 1958), 128.)

58. J. M. Robinson, ed., *The Nag Hammadi Library in English,* 195–205.
59. E. S. Fiorenza, "Word, Spirit and Power," in R. Ruether and E. McLaughlin, eds. *Women of Spirit* (New York: Simon and Schuster, 1979), 50.

Chapter 11. Retrospect and Prospect: Eve and the Death of God

1. Paula Fredriksen Landes, in *Signs: A Journal of Women in Culture and Society* 6, no. 2 (Winter 1980): 329.
2. Ibid., 334.
3. Erich Fromm, *You Shall Be As Gods* (New York: Holt, Rinehart & Winston, 1966).
4. M. Finley, "Archaeology and History," *Daedelus* 100, no. 1 (Winter, 1971): 168–186; S. B. Pomeroy, *Goddesses, Whores, Wives and Slaves: Women in Classical Antiquity* (New York: Schocken Books, 1975), 14.
5. D. L. Carmody, *Feminism and Christianity,* (Nashville, Tenn.: Abingdon, 1982).

Selected Bibliography

Chapter 1

Cassuto, Umberto. *A Commentary on the Book of Genesis*, pt. 1. Jerusalem: Magnes Press, Hebrew University, 1961.

Ginzberg, Louis. *Legends of the Jews*. Vol. 1, Philadelphia: Jewish Publication Society of America, 1909.

Graves, Robert, and Patai, Raphael. *Hebrew Myths: The Book of Genesis*. New York: McGraw Hill, 1964.

Heidel, Alexander. *The Babylonian Genesis*. 2d ed. Chicago: University of Chicago Press, 1951.

Patai, Raphael, *The Hebrew Goddess*. Philadelphia: KTAV, 1976.

Pritchard, James B., ed. *Ancient Near Eastern Texts Relating to the Old Testament*. 3d ed. Princeton, N. J.: Princeton University Press, 1969.

Trible, Phyllis. "Depatriarchalizing in Biblical Interpretation." In *The Jewish Woman: New Perspectives*. New York: Schocken Books, 1972.

Vawter, Bruce. *On Genesis*. New York: Doubleday, 1977.

Westermann, Claus. *Genesis 1–12*. Darmstadt, West Germany: Wissenschaftliche Buchgesellschaft, 1972.

Chapter 2

Evelyn-White, H. G., ed. *Hesiod: Works and Days*. Cambridge, England: McGraw-Hill, 1950.

Graves, Robert. *The Greek Myths*. Vol. 1. New York: McGraw-Hill, 1955.

Graves, Robert. *The Greek Myths*. Vol. 2. New York: McGraw-Hill, 1955.

Harrison, Jane E. "Pandora's Box." *Journal of Hellenic Studies* 20 (1900): 99–144.

Lattimore, Richard, ed. *Hesiod: Works and Days and Theogony*. Ann Arbor, Mich.: University of Michigan Press, 1959.

Neumann, Erich. *The Great Mother*. Princeton, N. J.: 1963.

Panofsky, Dora, and Panofsky, Erwin. *Pandora's Box: Changing Aspects of a Mythological Symbol*. New York: Pantheon, 1962.

Schwarz, Paul. *Die Neue Eva*. Göppingen, West Germany: Kümmerle, 1973.

Chapter 3

Evans. J. M. *Paradise Lost and the Genesis Tradition.* Oxford, England: Clarendon Press, 1968.

Freedman, H., and Simon, M., eds. *Midrash Rabba: Genesis I.* London: Soncino Press, 1939.

Rodkinson, M. L., trans. *The Talmud.* New York: New Amsterdam Book Co., 1901-1903.

Chapter 4

Charles, R. H., ed. *The Apocrypha and Pseudepigrapha of the Old Testament.* Vol. 2, *Pseudepigrapha.:* 1913. Oxford: The Clarendon Press.

Gaster, T. H. *Myth, Legend and Custom in the Old Testament.* New York: Harper & Row, 1969.

Rappoport, A. S., and Patai, R. *Myth and Legend in Ancient Israel,* vol. 1. Philadelphia: KTAV, 1966.

Reik, Theodore. *Myth and Guilt.* New York: Braziller, 1970.

Scholem, Gershom. "Lilith." In Cecil Roth, ed., *Encyclopedia Judaica.* New York: Macmillan, 1971.

Williams, N. P. *Ideas of the Fall and Original Sin.* London: Longmans, Green and Co., 1927.

Chapter 5

Kramer, H., and Sprenger, J. *Malleus Malificarum.* Translated by Montague Summers. London: Pushkin Press, 1951.

Milton, John. *Christian Doctrine.* In *Complete Prose Works of John Milton,* vol. 6. New Haven, Conn.: Yale University Press, 1973.

von Rad, Gerhard. *Genesis.* Philadelphia: Westminster, 1971.

Chapter 6

Fromm, Eric. *You Shall Be As Gods.* New York: Holt, Rinehart and Winston, 1966.

Levy, Ludwig. "Sexual Symbolik in der biblischer Paradisgeschichte." *Imago* 5 (1917-1919): 8-26.

Roheim, Geza. "The Garden of Eden." *Psychoanalytic Review* vol. 27 no. 2 (January 1940): 1-26, 177-199.

Chapter 7

Barth, Karl. *Church Dogmatics,* vol. I/3. Edinburgh, Scotland: T. & T. Clark, 1955 f.

Barth, Karl. *Church Dogmatics,* vol. III/2. Edinburgh, Scotland: T. & T. Clark 1955 f.

Barth, Karl. *Church Dogmatics,* vol. III/4. Edinburgh, Scotland: T. & T. Clark, 1969.

Frye, Northrop. *The Return of Eden.* Toronto: University of Toronto Press, 1965.

Le Comte, Edward. *Milton and Sex.* New York: Columbia University Press, 1978.

Milton, John. *Paradise Lost.* In Carey, J., and Fowler, A., eds., *The Poems of John Milton.* London: Longmans, 1968.

Patrides, C. A. *Milton and the Christian Tradition.* Oxford, England: Clarendon Press, 1966.

Chapter 8

Barrett, C. K. *A Commentary on the First Epistle to the Corinthians.* New York: Harper & Row, 1968.

Scroggs, Robin. "Paul and the Eschatological Woman." *Journal of the American Academy of Religion* 40, no. 3 (Sept. 1972).

Stanton, Elizabeth Cady, et al. *The Woman's Bible.* Ca. 1895–1898; reprint, Seattle, Wash.: Coalition Task Force on Woman and Religion, 1974.

Chapter 9

Ashe, Geoffrey. *The Virgin.* London: Routledge and Kegan Paul, 1976.

de Satgé, John. *Mary and the Christian Gospel* London: SPCK, 1976.

Warner, Marina. *Alone of All Her Sex.* New York: Knopf, 1976.

Chapter 10

Ali, Syed Ameer. "Fatima." In *A Shorter Encyclopedia of Islam.* Edited by Leiden, The Netherlands: E. J. Brill, 1953.

Bugge, John. *Virginitas: An Essay in the History of a Medieval Ideal.* The Hague, Netherlands: Martinus Nijhoff, 1975.

Fiorenza, E. S. "Word, Spirit and Power." In Reuther, R., and McLaughlin, E., eds. *Women of Spirit.* New York: Simon and Schuster, 1979.

Grant, R. M., ed. *Gnosticism.* New York: Harper & Row, 1961.

Robinson, James, ed. *The Nag Hammadi Library in English.* San Francisco: Harper & Row, 1977.

MacRae, G. W. "The Jewish Background of the Gnostic Sophia Myth." *Novum Testamentum* 12 (1969): 86–101.

Mernissi, Fatima. *Beyond the Veil.* Cambridge, Mass.: Schenkman Publishing Co., 1975.

Pagels, Elaine. *The Gnostic Gospels.* New York: Random House. 1977.

Scholem, Gershom. *Major Trends in Jewish Mysticism.* New York: Schocken Books, 1954.

Stead, G. C. "The Valentinian Myth of Sophia." *Journal of Theological Studies* 20 (April 1969): 75–104.

Vaglieri, L. Veccia. "Fatima." In B. Lewis, Ch. Pellat, and J. Schacht, eds. *The Encyclopedia of Islam.* Vol. 2. 2nd ed. London: Luzac & Co., 1965.

Illustrations

Anderson, Wayne. *Gauguin's Paradise Lost.* New York: Viking, 1971.

Dorra, Henri. "The First Eves in Gauguin's Eden." *Gazette des Beaux-Arts* 41 (Paris, 1953): 182–202.

Kirschbaum, Engelbert. "Adam und Eva." *Lexikon der Christlichen Ikonographie.* Vol. 1 Freiburg, West Germany: Herder, 1968.

Reáu, Louis. "La Creátion du Monde." "La Chute." *Iconographie de L'art Chretién.* Vol. 2. Paris: Presses Universitaires de France, 1956.

Steinberg, Leo. "Eve's Idle Hand." *Art Journal* 35, no. 2 (Winter 1975–1976).

Steinberg, Leo. "The Line of Fate in Michelangelo's Paintings." *Critical Inquiry* 6, no. 3 (Spring 1960).

Index of Authors

Albertus Magnus, 187
Ali Syed, Ameer, 188
Anderson, Wayne, 163
Anselm, St., 146
Anthony, St., 168
Anthony, Susan B., 56, 168
Aquinas, Thomas, 28, 35, 59, 179,
    180, 182, 183, 184
Aristotle, 35, 180
Ashe, Geoffrey, 178, 187
Auerbach, Eric, 58, 182
Augustine, 14, 28, 36, 44, 59, 64,
    65–66, 75–76, 89, 143, 182, 183
Avitus, 59

Babrius, 19
Barrett, C. K., 124, 125, 187
Barth, Karl, 106, 108, 109, 110, 112,
    113, 114, 115, 185, 186
Bernard of Clairvaux, 187
Boccaccio, Giovanni, 179
Bonnell, J. K., 62, 182
Brown, N. O., 178, 180
Brown, R. E., 187
Bugge, John, 189
al-Bukhari, 188
Bulgakov, Sergei, 187

Calvin, John, 99, 102, 104, 105, 106,
    108, 110, 115, 180, 183, 185
Campbell, Joseph, 83
Carmody, D. L., 176, 190
Cassuto, Umberto, 60, 74, 177, 180,
    182, 183
Celsus, 21, 79
Christ, Carol, 177
Cyril of Alexandria, 139

Daly, Mary, 56, 180, 182, 186, 188
Dante Alighieri, 39, 59, 126, 143,
    181, 182, 186, 188
Dillmann, August, 81, 184

Dorra, Henri, 163
Dracontius, 33, 35, 36, 180, 182
Dworkin, Andrea, 95, 185

Epiphanius, 168, 189
Erasmus, Desiderius, 23
Erhart, Michael, 137
Evans, J. M., 102, 181, 182, 183, 185,
    186

Findlay, M., 190
Fiorenza, Elizabeth S., 169, 190
Foerster, Werner, 189
Ford, J. M., 187
Fowler, A., 185
France, Anatole, 44
Freud, Sigmund, 14, 87–89, 93, 160,
    184
Fromm, Erich, 91, 175, 177, 185, 190
Frye, Northrup, 102, 185

Gaster, T. H., 181
al-Ghazali, 154
Ginzberg, Louis, 178, 179, 180, 182,
    183, 184, 186
Goldziher, Ignaz, 150, 188
Gossaert, Jan, 111
Graef, Hilda, 187
Grant, R. M., 189
Graves, Robert, 19, 177, 178, 180,
    186
Gregory of Nazianzus, 22, 106, 186
Gregory of Nyssa, 182
Gressmann, Hugo, 180, 184
Grotius, Hugo, 183
Gunkel, Hermann, 177, 184

Harnack, Adolf von, 189, 190
Hefele, K. J. von, 187
Heidel, Alexander, 177
al-Hassan, Abu, 180
Herder, J. G. von, 80

Hesiod, 16, 19, 20, 21, 22, 35, 84, 177, 178
Hooker, D. M., 124, 125

Irenaeus, 133, 184, 187, 189

Jeremias, Alfred, 177
Jerome, St., 146, 168, 187, 188
Joshua of Siknin, 29
Jung, C. G., 85, 87, 114, 165
Justin, 162
Justin Martyr, St., 133, 187

Kant, Immanuel, 80
Katsivelos, Elizabeth, 183
Kikawada, Isaac, 3, 177
Köhler, Ludwig, 177
Kramer, Heinrich, 182, 183

Landes, Paula, 172, 174, 190
Le Comte, Edward, 185
Lederer, Wolfgang, 95, 185
Levy, Ludwig, 90, 185
Lowell, Robert, 72, 183
Luther, Martin, 58, 98, 102, 104, 105, 108, 110, 115, 182, 185

MacRae, George, 163, 165, 187, 189
Maimonides, Moses, 79, 184
Maurus, Hrabanus, 179
Mernissi, Fatima, 154, 188
Methodius, St., 146
Mieggi, Giovanni, 187
Millet, Kate, 177
Milton, John, 9, 33, 34, 36, 59, 66, 72, 74, 101, 102, 105, 180, 182, 183, 185
al-Mulk, Nizan, 150

Neumann, Erich, 20, 87, 144, 178, 181, 184

Oliver, Jean, 179

Pagels, Elaine, 166, 177, 186, 189
Panofsky, Dora and Erwin, 178, 179
Parrinder, Geoffrey, 188
Patai, Raphael, 39, 177, 178, 180, 181, 186, 187, 188, 189
Patrides, C. A., 180
Pearson, B. A., 189

Philo Judaeus (of Alexandria), 30, 50, 162, 165, 180, 182
Philodemus, 19
Pomeroy, S. B., 190

Rad, Gerhard von, 61, 182
Rank, Otto, 87, 89, 93, 138
Rashi, 181
Reik, Theodore, 23, 45, 179, 181, 183
Robinson, H. Wheeler, 177
Robinson, James M., 189
Roheim, Geza, 89–95, 160, 180, 185
Russell, J. B., 178, 184

Sachs, Hans, 181
de Satgé, John, 187
Schiller, J. C. F. von, 78, 80, 184
Scholem, Gershom, 158, 159, 180, 188, 189
Schopenhauer, Arthur, 19
Schuon, Frithjof, 188
Schwarz, Paul, 21, 42, 74, 83, 150, 178, 181, 182, 183, 184, 188
Scroggs, Robin, 120–127, 186
Shakespeare, William, 143
Smith, Ronald Gregor, 13
Spenser, Edmund, 10, 44, 143, 177
Sprenger, James, 182, 183
Stanton, Elizabeth Cady, 126, 187
Stead, G. C., 162, 165, 189
Steinberg, Leo, 25, 67, 179, 183, 187
Sweet, John, 187

Tertullian, 21, 44, 50, 124, 134, 179, 183, 186, 187
de Tolnay, Charles, 183
Trible, Phyllis, 10, 110, 177, 180, 185, 186

Vaglieri, L. V., 188
Vawter, Bruce, 40, 45, 55, 179, 181, 182

Walker, William O., 186
Wellhausen, Julius, 81, 184
Westermann, Claus, 14, 115, 178, 184, 186
Williams, N. P., 181

Zuckoff, Aviva Cantor, 181

Index of Subjects

Abel, 46, 68
Abraham, 152
Umm Abiha, 153
Adam, 10, 13, 25, 26, 27, 28, 29, 30, 33, 34, 36, 38, 39, 43, 44, 49, 50, 55, 57, 58, 62, 64, 72, 74, 75, 76, 77, 80, 89, 90, 91, 93, 99, 101, 102, 104, 105, 106, 109, 110, 117, 120, 121, 144, 148, 149, 164, 167, 170; as God's image, 57; character of, 36, 49, 50, 58, 74, 76, 93, 106; sentence upon, 77, 90, 120, 121; solitude of, 30, 32, 33, 34
Adam and Eve, 27, 28, 30, 34, 46, 57, 65, 66, 72, 75, 79, 83, 86, 91, 92, 100, 101, 103, 107, 109, 111, 119, 125, 143, 152, 155, 159, 162; wedding of, 27, 28
adamah, 13, 27
Adamites, 67
Ahriman, 155
Ali, 153
Allah, 149, 150, 152, 154
almah, 132
analogia relationis, 108
Anath, 156
Aphrodite, 4
arummim, 181
Asherah, 156
Astarte, 40, 156

Beckmann, Max, 23, 82, 86
bene ha-elohim. *See* Watcher Angels
al-Biruni, 155
Bosch, Hieronymous, 63
box, as vagina, 23
brahmacharya, 168

Cain, 46, 68
Canaanite deities, 12
Christ, 50, 79, 104, 120, 121, 123, 135, 146, 167, 171

Church Fathers, 16, 21, 22, 23, 44, 45, 50, 80, 133, 135, 143, 144
Council of Ephesus, 139
covenant, 11, 14, 109, 170
Cranach, Lucas, 73, 103
Creation: and civilization, 13, 14, 157; *ex nihilo*, 5, 6, 13; myths, Babylonian, 5, 7, 8; myths, Canaanite, 8; myths, Greek, 4, 5; myths, Hebrew, 5, 7; myths, Mesopotamian, 7; myths, Near Eastern, 4, 5, 7, 10, 138, 170; order of, 27; Priestly account of, 13, 27; Yahwist account of, 27
"Creation of Adam," by Michelangelo, 25, 131, 134
"Creation of Eve," by Michelangelo, 25, 27, 31, 33, 44
Cronos, 20
Cupid, 73

Death, illustrated, 9
Death of God theology, 176
demon-eve tradition, 44, 45, 51
depatriarchalizing exegesis, 10
devekuth, 158
Devil, 19, 55, 58, 62, 64, 138, 159. *See also* Satan
divorce, 104, 113
dragon-mother. *See* Tiamat
Dürer, Albrecht, 34

Eden, Garden of, xv, 19, 37, 39, 41, 42, 46, 49, 50, 55, 64, 78, 80, 81, 84, 87, 89, 90, 101, 104, 110, 115, 147, 149, 150; politics of, 101, 147
eisegesis, xv
Elohim, 11, 162
Enlightenment, 78, 80, 83, 89, 90
Epimetheus, 17, 19, 23, 37
Essenes, 51

Eve: and veil, 120; as adviser (or instructor), 164, 166; as God's image, 42, 57; as thief, 29; attributes of, 33–34, 35, 36; character of, 33, 34, 35, 36, 38, 49, 50, 58, 64, 78, 93, 106, 132, 135, 145; creation of, 25, 27, 28, 30, 35, 41, 45, 89; curiosity of, 38, 59, 63, 77; greed of, 59, 62, 77; hand of, 68, 69; imagination of, 61; irrationality of, 61; meaning of name of, 3, 22, 28, 29, 40, 41, 165, 166; relationship to Satan, 41, 45, 61, 62, 64, 67, 72; relationship to serpent, 25, 37, 38, 41, 42, 55, 61, 64, 67, 68, 93; sensuality of, 22, 44, 61, 62, 64, 74, 77, 99; sentence against, 76, 77, 89, 101, 105, 115, 117, 133, 143, 147, 183; shadow side of, 39, 50; vanity of, 22, 59, 62; weakness of, 57, 74

evil impulse. *See yetzer-ha-ra*

exousia, 123, 124

van Eyck, Hubert, 119

van Eyck, Jan, 119

ezer, 27, 32, 109, 110, 165

Fall, 14, 22, 39, 41, 45, 46, 47, 61, 78, 80, 81, 83, 84, 89, 90, 91, 93, 94, 100, 101, 102, 104, 108, 115, 126, 133, 134–135, 142, 143, 159; and civilization, 89, 78–81, 91, 93, 94; as sexual 45, 62, 64, 84, 89, 90, 143; as alienation, 108; as *felix culpa*, 78–79, 80, 91, 93, 94; as technological, 46, 47; as universal story, 83

fallen angels. *See* Watcher Angels

Fatima, 152 ff.

Feminine, as religious concept, 3, 4, 15, 20, 140, 142, 154, 155, 164, 165, 171

fica, 68

fitna, 154, 188

Flaxman, John, 48

forbidden fruit, 27, 41, 61, 62, 67, 74, 83, 86, 183; as apple, 68, 84; as fig, 68; as Eve's breast, 85, 86, 90; and knowledge, 89

Gabriel, Archangel, 132, 133, 134

Gâdreêl, 47

Gandhi, Mohandas K., 168

Gauguin, Paul, 88, 94, 163

God, 3, 4, 5, 6, 7, 8, 11, 12, 13, 14, 27, 32, 34, 89, 93, 95, 99, 104, 105, 108, 109, 114, 148, 152, 155, 156, 157, 159, 160; and history, 12, 14; and nature, 12, 14; and technology, 12, 13; and relationality, 108; *aseitas* of, 114; feminine aspects of, 11, 152, 156, 159, 160, 162; image of, 27, 34, 99, 104, 108, 113; in Judaism, 11, 12; independence of, 6; masculinity of, 4, 6, 7, 8, 11, 33, 148, 155, 156; ninety-nine names of, 152, 156; oneness of, 5, 6, 7, 8, 115, 155, 157; relation to creation of, 5, 6, 13

goddess, 3, 5, 7; as good/bad, 84

Great Mother archetype, 85–86

Grien, Hans Baldung, 86, 92

gynocide, 117

hadith, xvi, 150, 152, 171

hallah, 29

Hanya tribe, 84

Ḥawwāh, 3, 40, 41, 165–166

al-Hayawan, Manafi, 151

helper (helpmeet), 27, 32, 101, 106, 109, 112

Hephaistos, 16, 17, 20

Hera, 20

Hermes, 19

hiwya, 41

Holy Spirit, 156

homosexuality, 114

Ialdabaoth, 162, 164

Iblis, 41, 149. *See also* Satan, Devil

idology, 175

incest, 89–95

Innocent VIII, Pope, 70

ish, 27, 179

ishshah, 27, 32, 179

Isis cult, 162

Islam, 149–155, 156, 169

Israel, 12, 14, 157

Jesus, 114, 121, 132, 135, 136, 138, 152, 166

Kabbalah, 36, 157, 158, 159, 160, 169

kalon kakon, 17, 20, 21

Klee, Paul, 23

Klinger, Max, 60

Lady of Life, 28
Lady of the Rib, 28
"Last Judgment," by Michelangelo, 67, 69
Leviathan (Lothan), 7, 8, 138
Lilith, 39, 40, 41, 51, 72, 142, 144, 158, 159, 180
Limbourg Brothers, 63
Lippi, Filippino, 68
logos, 165
Lucifer, 36

Maitani, Lorenzo, 31
Mahdi, 153
Manichaeism, 43, 89
Marduk, 5, 6, 8, 10, 13
marriage, 104, 112, 113, 114, 115, 123, 147
Mariology, 117, 132, 135–136, 139, 140, 143, 146, 148, 153, 171. See also Virgin Mary
menstruation, 29, 88, 183
Mesopotamia, culture of, 12, 32
Michael, Archangel, 138
Michelangelo, 25, 27, 31, 44, 67, 68, 69, 71, 134
Miriam. See Virgin Mary
mitmenschlichkeit, 108
Moses, 21, 81, 152
Mother Goddess, 3–13, 14, 41, 87, 140, 142, 175, 176; worship of, 7, 176; death of, 7, 170, 175, 176
Mother of All Believers, 144
Mother of All the Living, 3, 4, 13, 15, 28, 40, 141, 144, 148, 164, 165, 171
Mozart, Wolfgang A., 108
al-Muhaddatha, 153
Muhammad, 114, 152, 153

Naccherino, Michelangelo, 75
naming, as power, 32
natural law, 147
Neo-Platonism, 162
New Adam. See Second Adam
New Eve. See Second Eve
Nolde, Emil, 173

Oedipal situation, 87, 89, 90
Olympians, 5, 20
Onesimus, 123
Ophites, 43, 79, 162

Pan, 19
Pandora, 16, 17, 18, 19, 20, 21, 23, 35, 36–37, 45, 51, 58, 78, 84, 143, 177, 179; meaning of name, 17, 19, 70
Pandora's Box, 23
parthenos, 132
patriarchalism, 10, 11
Paul, Apostle, 50, 58, 74, 110, 115, 120, 121, 122, 123, 124
Philemon, 123
pithos, 17, 20, 23
Priestly account, 12, 27, 30, 38
Priestly writer, 12, 42
Prince of Demons. See Satan
Prometheus, 16, 17, 21, 78
proto-eves, 38, 39, 41
prostitution, sacred, 142, 146
Pseudo Met de Bles, 63
Pythagorean, 162
pyxis, 23

quaid, 154
Queen of Heaven, 156
della Quercia, Jacopo, 26, 65

Rahab, 7, 8
rape, 32
rasul, 152
Rembrandt, 107
Rhea, 20
rib, 16, 25, 28, 30, 35, 38, 45
Rizzo, Antonio, 116
Rousseau, Henri, 43

Samael, 36, 41, 158, 159, 164
Sâmjâza, 47
Satan, 9, 36, 42, 45, 49, 57, 58, 61, 62, 64, 67, 72, 75, 89, 138, 139, 149, 160, 168
Shaitan, 41
Satona, 50
Satomail, 50
Second Adam, 50, 106, 118, 120, 121, 122, 123, 133, 136
Second Eve, 25, 122, 131, 134, 136, 137, 139, 152, 171; Virgin Mary as, 131ff., 169
Second Vatican Council, 136
Sefira, sefiroth, 157; 159
serpent, 8, 25, 35, 41, 44, 45, 55, 57, 61–62, 63, 64, 68, 75, 79, 89, 133, 134, 138, 149, 166; and sexuality,

44; and wisdom, 41; as adviser, 149, 166; as benefactor, 79; as female, 25, 61–62; with female head, 63, 68, 75

serpent-mother, 41, 165

Seth, 49

Sethian, 162

Sin, 9, 37, 157; doctrine of original sin, 65, 143

sharia, 150

Shi'a, Shi'ites, 149, 153, 154, 169

shirk, 152

Shekhina, 157, 158, 159, 164

Sodoma, 125

"sons of God." *See* Watcher Angels

Sophia, 124, 162, 163, 164, 165, 166

Sophia-Zoe, 124, 164

Sunni, 152, 153

syzygia, 167, 168, 169

"tail," woman as, 42, 181

tehom, 5, 7, 8

"Temptation and Expulsion," by Michelangelo, 25, 67–68, 70, 71

Tiamat, 5, 7, 8, 10, 15, 41, 143, 144

tohu-wa-bohu, 5

Torah, 146, 157

tree of knowledge, 55

Trinity, 109, 139, 162

tsela, 28

Uranians, 5

Valentinians, 124, 162, 165, 167

veil, 50, 120, 121, 123, 124, 126, 154

Venus, 23

virgin, etymology of, 142

Virgin Mary, 131, 132–134, 136, 138, 139, 140, 143, 145, 153 (*see also* Mariology); as Mother of All Believers, 136; as Mother of God, 140; as Queen of Heaven, 140; as Second Eve, 131, 132, 134, 139, 140, 143, 145; as Woman Clothed with the Sun, 138–139, 140; bodily

assumption of, 136; immaculate conception of, 136; perpetual virginity of, 136, 140; virginity of, 133, 134, 135, 136, 141–142, 143, 144, 145, 146

Virgin Mother, 145, 146, 147

virginity, 132, 134, 135, 136, 141, 143, 144, 146, 168

Voltaire, 23

Watcher Angels, 45, 46, 47, 48, 50, 64

Wiligelmo, 26

Wisdom, 156, 162, 163, 165

wisdom, and serpents, 41

witch, witchcraft, 39, 47, 62, 70–71, 143

wives, subjection of, 104

Woman: and death, 84, 87, 95, 143, 167; and the demonic, 9; and evil, 9, 17, 21, 22, 118; and nonexistence, 44, 87, 93; and serpents, 9, 41, 45, 51, 89; as helpmeet, 112–113; as seducer, 44; character of, 10, 22, 23, 64, 70–71, 84; clothed with the sun, 138 f., 141, 152; curiosity of, 21, 23, 58, 59; etymology of name, 27, 32; eschatological, 122, 126; sensuality of, 49, 51, 64, 70; veiling of, 50, 121, 123, 124, 126, 154

Yahweh, 3, 4, 5, 8, 10, 11, 12, 13, 14, 40, 46, 79, 157, 162, 170

Yahwist, 27, 28, 32, 40, 41, 45, 46, 57, 59, 72, 74, 89, 91, 93, 115, 139, 181

Yahwist account, 30, 38

yetzer-ha-ra, 36, 45, 46

al-Zahra, 153

Zeus, 16, 17, 18, 20, 21, 178

Zoë, 124

Zoroastrian, 155, 189

Index of Literature Cited in Text

Adam, Apocalypse of, 189
Adam and Eve, Books of, 16, 49, 50
Apocrypha, 46

Baruch, 46, 50
Baruch (Gnostic), 162

Chester Plays, 62

Dialogue of the Savior, 189

Egyptians, Apocryphal Gospel of, 168
Enoch, Apocalypse of (Ethiopic Enoch,
    Enoch I), 16, 42
Enoch, Secrets of (Slavonic Enoch, Enoch
    II), 50
Enûma Elish, 5, 7, 13, 15, 144, 177
Eve, Gospel of, 50
Exegesis on the Soul, 162, 166

Hermetica, 80, 184
Historia Libri Genesis, 62, 77
Hypostasis of the Archons, 164

John, Apocryphon of, 162, 163, 164
Jubilees, 47, 50

Libellus, 184

Malleus Maleficarum, 70, 182, 183
Midrash Rabba (Genesis), 29, 30, 180,
    181, 186
Moses, Apocalypse of, 16
Mystere d' Adam, 58

Nag Hammadi Library, 161, 187, 188,
    189, 190
New Testament, xvi
Noah, Book of, 47

On the Origins of the World, 164, 188

Paradise Lost (Milton), 9, 33, 59, 72,
    102
Philip, Gospel of, 167

Qur'an, xvi, 6, 7, 41, 149, 150, 152,
    171

Scrolls, Dead Sea, 51
Secrets of Enoch. See Enoch, Secrets of
Seth, Second Treatise of, 162
Sirach, 46, 49, 50
Sophia of Jesus Christ, 124, 187
Stromata II, 189

Talmud, xvi, 148, 165, 171, 181
Testament of Reuben, 49, 50
Testament of the 12 Patriarchs, 49
Thomas, Gospel of, 166
The Thunder, Perfect Mind, 164

Valentinian Exposition, 166

Wisdom, 46, 50
Woman's Bible, The, 126–127
Works and Days (Hesiod), 16

Zohar, 157, 158